HR Leadershift

Sarah -
Make a difference

- differently.

HR Leadershift

The Five Distinctions of a Strategic HR Leader

Sara Christiansen

With a Foreword by Laura Lee

CLEARSIGHT
BOOKS

Raleigh, North Carolina

ISBN hardback: 978-1-945209-13-0
ISBN paperback: 978-1-945209-14-7
ISBN ebook: 978-1-945209-15-4

Library of Congress Control Number: 2021907452

For bulk purchases of this book or for information about workshops based
on this book, visit hrleadershift.com.

Published by Clear Sight Books, Raleigh, North Carolina

Contents

I would like to dedicate this book to all the essential workers who weave the fabric of our country. Your dedication is often overlooked and minimized. But I see you. I appreciate you. I watch you serve with honor. This past year you have sacrificed your time, your talents and some of you even your lives for the greater good. We owe you an unrepayable debt of gratitude.

Foreword

Sara Christiansen is a well-respected human resources thought leader who helps companies and HR professionals drive and improve organizational performance. She shares her expertise globally and has worked alongside other internationally known leaders and best-selling authors, such as Marcus Buckingham and Cy Wakeman. Throughout her career, Sara has been at the forefront of innovation, consistently working to improve the HR profession. No matter how long you have been practicing human resources, you can always learn something new from Sara.

Having the honor to read the *HR Leadershift* manuscript, I was amazed at Sara's insights and observations, which show how HR has never been more influential or important. As leaders in human resources, our role is to guide the design and implementation of the work options needed to fuel growth. We and our teams must demonstrate agility as we architect new business initiatives for our organization's future. This book is rich with examples of organizations that have embraced the fast-changing world of work with robust and visionary HR leadership. Digitization in the workplace is accelerating, and the HR role is becoming increasingly critical. As *strategic* HR leaders, we are evolving to imagine, invent, and ignite our organizations to change. Human capital strength will be what differentiates a business's long-term success or failure. By reading Sara's book, you will learn strategies to improve your journey as a strategic human resources leader.

I look forward to Sara's book being published and sharing it with my team. Her knowledge of the HR field and wisdom as a strategic leader is imparted on every page and will be of great benefit to any HR professional.

—*Laura Lee, CHRO, MGM Resorts International*

INTRODUCTION

The entire world has recently changed drastically. I am writing this in the midst of a nationwide lockdown due to the COVID-19 pandemic. The future is quite uncertain, the economy has been intentionally shut down, and we have lost hundreds of thousands of American lives. Businesses are scurrying to develop best practices for reopening the doors. Americans are having to rethink everything. How do we protect our communities and our incomes? How do we open the economy without triggering a resurgence of infections? How do we plan for a *new normal*?

In the June 2020 issue of *Human Resource Executive Magazine*, I came across a great article written by Ben Brooks titled "A Crisis Is a Terrible Thing to Waste." The piece begins with the seemingly weird question, "What if COVID-19 is the most important thing to ever happen to HR?" Ben talks about how this pandemic has elevated HR to "unprecedented levels of visibility, importance and influence. Unlike ten to twenty years ago, you're not fighting for a seat at the table. You're leading the goddamn meeting . . . seize the moment."

In my career there have been several reality-changing events. On September 11, 2001, the world seemed to change in a few shocking moments. At 8 a.m. I was driving to my job at an agricultural (pork production) company in rural Minnesota (yes, I was running late as usual).

Prior to 9/11, my colleagues and I agreed that recruiting and staffing were the biggest challenges we were facing. So, as I pulled out of my driveway, I was increasingly excited for the promising interview that I had on my calendar later that morning. As I was contemplating the questions that I planned to ask this prospective manager, the radio DJ on a normally very funny morning show solemnly announced that a fire had broken out at the World Trade Center in New York City.

I instantly felt disappointment, as I had tickets to fly to New York City on Thursday. We were planning this trip to attend the wedding of a dear friend on Long Island on September 15. A visit to the World Trade Center was on our agenda for Friday. I remember being somewhat annoyed at the inconvenience this fire was causing me.

As I arrived in the office and was preparing for the interview, I looked up at the TV mounted in the lobby and saw the plane explode into the second tower. Those of you old enough will forever remember what you felt in that monumental moment. It seemed the world had stopped in an instant.

Millions around the world were watching the live coverage on morning news of what was theorized at the time to be a small plane that had accidently collided with the World Trade Center. At 9:20 a.m. on the East Coast, everything changed in a literal New York minute. The realization that this was something much more significant than a wayward Cessna instantaneously sparked a fear that most of us had never experienced.

Up until that day my generation had felt invincible. We lived in an America that we believed was essentially isolated from the tragedies of the world. We did not think about terrorism. That was the work best left to our elected officials. Call us naive, but we felt protected by the oceans between us and turmoil. The only understanding I had of Middle East conflict was memories of Wolf Blitzer hiding under a desk in Baghdad, describing the dominance of the coalition forces over the Iraqi regime that had recently invaded Kuwait. That was the extent of my awareness. I had never heard the name Osama bin Laden. I had no knowledge of the Taliban and their anti-American ideologies.

But in that moment, we witnessed our true vulnerability with our own eyes. This was not a foreign military's act of war. This was a terrorist attack on citizens in an iconic American landmark. This was an attack on our economy. An attack on democracy. An attack on our lifestyle. An attack on our sense of security.

However, every crisis provides opportunities for learning. Opportunities for amazing displays of humanity. Opportunities for great leadership.

Through this experience I changed my views about leadership. Prior to this, I had gladly promoted the merits of professionalism—business jargon for hiding your emotions. I thought that leaders needed to stay cool and collected in every situation and leave their personal stuff at home every day. HR spent a lot of sweat and tears over defining leadership competencies such as grit or steadfastness. At the time, qualities like authenticity, vulnerability, emotional intelligence, humility, and benevolence never made the list.

However, in the days that followed 9/11 I was riveted by the response of community and business leaders in New York. With this horrendous human tragedy, I expected leaders to show strength by stepping up and taking charge. And although we saw the president do just that, on my TV I witnessed something profound. Many big, strong, proud firefighters broke down in tears as they shared stories of fallen brethren. I watched heart-wrenching interviews with a devastated Howard Lutnick, the CEO of Cantor Fitzgerald, after losing 658 employees in the towers. I watched newscasters taking a minute to regain their composure. I saw everyday citizens perform miracles of courage and compassion. What I witnessed has changed my thoughts about leadership to this day.

Another monumental moment in my career occurred in August 2005. I was a corporate senior HR manager with a global organization when Hurricane Katrina hit the Gulf Coast with Category 5 forces. The real devastation occurred when the levees in New Orleans gave way. The entire region suffered deadly flooding. Eventually, 80 percent of the city was inundated for weeks, as were large tracts of neighboring parishes. The death toll exceeded 1,800.

My company had two offices located in New Orleans. As the storm developed and flood levels were rising, many employees informed me that they were unable to contact our NOLA offices. We did not know the fate of our employees, our customers, or our property in the area.

I learned that HR needs to be adaptable and rise to any unforeseen occasion. Following Katrina, our corporate employees were terrified, and many were asking me what they should do. How was I to know? There was no procedure for this. There was no one to ask "What did we do last time?"

The storm did not give us the luxury of planning ahead. Thousands were homeless, many were stranded and dying in the aftermath, and the government seemed incapable (or unwilling) to bring rapid aid. This tragedy was happening to our fellow Americans and the 24-hour news media told the whole story. Most in the organization were looking to HR to provide a sense that it was going to be okay. They needed us to have the foresight to lead the leaders.

I had to think on my feet and respond in real time. HR became the emotional outlet for many on our teams. Sometimes we just needed to listen. Other times, we needed to provide answers to questions. But mostly we comforted those who were unsettled by the possibility of such a tragedy.

I recently had an amazing conversation with Amy Dufrane, the CEO of HRCI, about the impact of COVID-19. Although she was in the DC area and I was in Minnesota, we shared the same anxieties about the rapidly changing reality.

I commented to Amy, "HR will need to adapt and learn on the fly."

She nodded in agreement. "This is the call to action that HR has needed for a long time, in my opinion. And I think it is illustrating the necessity for Strategic HR at its core. I have talked to several CHROs who are in strategic roles who were prepared and ready, as ready as they could be. None of us were truly ready, but they were able to hold a business conversation that was rooted in the need—from an analytical perspective, from a business perspective—to be able to articulate the foundations for what is necessary in moving the business forward. So I think HR leaders who were not thinking strategically were caught seriously off guard and found themselves leading teams that were focused on the very tactical components of HR, which is not moving the business forward."

Amy and I went on to discuss the role of HR during this time. She talked about HR finding the gravitas to have conversations with senior leaders about how the business needs to change. She explained, "This COVID-19 situation illustrated the fact that a lot of people weren't ready strategically to handle what needed to be done."

When I spoke about the need for HR to learn how to better navigate uncharted waters, Amy agreed. "Transformative leadership is essential. That ability to be nimble and agile is essential. All the other things you can figure out, all the operational pieces. But the strategic pieces are the pieces that you need to have as an HR leader, not even in tomorrow's world; it's today's world. Tomorrow is here."

Tomorrow *is* here. In this book, my goal is to help HR professionals be ready for it. In it, I'll share what Strategic HR really is, how to get a seat at the table, and the five distinctions of a Strategic HR Leader (based on my proprietary research).

After more than twenty years in the HR field, from tactical roles to strategic consulting to keynote speaking, I've never been more convinced that this is the time for HR to step into its power and take a seat at the table.

A Seat at the Table

Recently I was having a conversation with the CHRO of a food company that employs over 12,000 people worldwide. We were engaged in a profound discussion about the current trends of HR transformation when he said something that took me by surprise. He prophesied, "HR will be obsolete in five years." I didn't fundamentally disagree with him, but it was shocking to hear this from a highly regarded HR leader.

His declaration resonated with me because I had been secretly fostering the same anxiety for quite a while; I just hadn't said it out loud. Over the past two decades I have defended the merits of HR to any professional who would listen. I have been a champion for our profession as we have evolved from the personnel office to highly competent business partners.

But my arguments seem increasingly baseless. We are at a crossroads. We can either continue to deny what is becoming obvious, or we can acknowledge the realities and forge a new path forward.

Despite all our efforts, I continue to hear countless stories of organizations that see HR as unnecessary overhead. Employees tell me that interacting with HR feels like they have been summoned to the principal's office. And many generalists are considering leaving HR because they are not allowed to make a true impact.

I am continually asked, "How do I get a seat at the table?" When I hear this question, I envision a silly scene in which there is a glorious conference table in the clouds covered in a gold lamé cloth and surrounded by beautiful thrones on which the anointed will sit and admire each other's shiny crown of jewels.

I do not know who originally coined the phrase "Strategic HR," but I would like to go back in time and change the course. Don't get me wrong; I believe that we are at our best when we serve as strategic business partners. But as a profession this term has damaged our credibility and created barriers to success. HR has been patiently waiting for an invitation to join the strategic process in hopes that we will be embraced and given our rightful place at the table.

Well, hang on to your hat, Willy Wonka. There is no golden ticket wrapped up nicely in your favorite chocolate bar. While we were waiting for our invitation, everyone else was looking for us to step up and contribute strategically. They really want you to be their strategic partner. But they did not realize they needed to send a formal invitation.

I often ask organizational leaders what they would wish for if they had a magic wand. Many tell me of their desires to have a team that understands people and can align talent with the organizational strategy. They want to learn how to attract the best and the brightest. They want help to establish a leadership pipeline that provides a foundation for sustained growth. They need support to foster an organizational culture that drives innovation and efficiency. They don't know to call this Strategic HR—they just know they want it.

Because we have not done a good job of defining and branding the concept of Strategic HR, we are not having discussions with our colleagues about what it might look like. In the absence of these conversations, HR professionals assume that there is not an appetite for their strategic contributions and quickly become disillusioned. This conflict of expectations has led to an HR identity crisis that lingers yet today.

HR is traditionally viewed as highly transactional. Over the last two decades our identity has become adversarial. We write and enforce the policies, we oversee employee discipline, we are the facilitators of most terminations, we make the unpopular wage decisions, and we communicate the increasing healthcare premium costs. Everyone loves to hate HR. And we hate that they hate us!

We see ourselves differently. We believe in doing the right thing and that usually means following a highly complicated statute. We are underpaid mini-lawyers who can recite employment law better than most DOL bureaucrats. If we make a mistake, the proverbial poo will hit the fan. We have all sat through countless audits, unemployment hearings and depositions, and conversations with lawyers. We all have stories of attending employment law seminars that preach cautionary tales that would terrify even the most seasoned executive.

But this is where we are missing the boat. Our obsession with risk mitigation is perpetuating our comparison to the Catholic school nuns with rulers. We talk the strategic game, but we walk a traditional and transactional game.

Which brings me back to the prediction of HR's eventual extinction. Collectively, our professional identity remains archaic.

We have been unable (or unwilling) to move our brand toward that of the strategic status we desire. As a result, I see our profession splitting into two camps.

There is one camp that revels in the traditional contributions of HR. They take great pride in their legal expertise. They are recruiting warriors and thrive during open enrollment season. They are fueled by the black and white of policy making. They are confident that their handbook and job descriptions are top notch. And they feel highly valued when managers come to HR for guidance around the progressive discipline process. They may want to be viewed as strategic, but honestly prefer to function from a traditional mindset. The beloved old dog–new tricks paradigm.

However, there is an emerging camp that is determined to forge an identity as a true strategic contributor. They resist having a traditional HR title because that may limit their perceived ability to have a strategic impact. Instead, they self-identify as organization development, or talent management, or learning and development, or employee experience, or people analytics . . . or, my new favorite, "workplace culture concierge." They are distancing themselves from HR to establish a new, truly strategic brand.

I recently spoke about this with Lyndsay Lord, the CHRO at Team Car Care (Jiffy Lube). She told me she describes herself as "a leader with an expertise in HR." She proudly stated that because she clearly understands the business drivers, she regularly *does not* stay in her lane.

Lyndsay also offered, "People dread Draconian HR. Being strategic is a given. The world is changing; how we work is changing. If we don't adapt, we won't have the right talent. Without talent, [the workplace] is just an empty building that doesn't produce any value." Her strategic philosophy is clear: you need the right people, doing the right thing, anchored to the right values. She asserted that the HR team at Jiffy Lube accomplishes this through "less mandating and more partnering" within Jiffy Lube's more than 550 stand-alone businesses.

As my CHRO friends and I realize, the traditional and transactional responsibilities performed by those firmly planted in the first camp are easily outsourced or automated. There are professional service providers that take care of payroll, benefit administration, recruiting, workers compensation, unemployment, audits, compliance reporting, communications, data storage, and many other tasks. These external partners can probably do it better and cheaper than in-house HR. And with the evolution of AI and other technologies, this trend is going to continue for the anticipated future. So, is it a forgone conclusion that HR will become obsolete?

I have been on an emotional journey trying to foresee the future for HR. Through the years I have developed a love for this work. HR is not just my profession; it is my passion. I believe that the pendulum has not swung so far that HR will cease to exist. However, the modern workplace is changing rapidly. The traditional HR model is unsustainable.

A few years ago, I was asked to assemble a discussion panel with professionals whom I considered to be strategic HR leaders. I pooled a list of names from my contacts and made some calls. Each person that I reached out to offered a similar response: "Thank you for asking me to participate; it is an honor that you have considered me. However, I do not think I am 'at the table.' I still have a long way to go to be considered strategic."

If *these* folks were unsure of their roles, I was afraid HR would never be considered as having a seat at the table.

It was then that I realized we didn't really have a benchmark or measuring stick to differentiate strategic human resources. There are many white papers and op-eds on the subject, but no real criteria against which to compare ourselves. It feels insincere to self-identify as "strategic" without a common understanding of what that entails.

The closest thing I had experienced to a definition of Strategic HR is the Human Resource Certification Institute's (HRCI) criteria for content. If you have been an HR professional for any length of time, you have undoubtedly been privy to conversations about the scarcity of HR programming that qualifies for the business credits required for the SPHR recertification. HRCI understandably has a very stringent process for a development program to be awarded these elevated credits. The content must meet a rigor of standards designed to ensure that the program covers learning objectives in the *SPHR Exam Content Outline* (HRCI.org):

"Leadership and Strategy Functional Area 01: Leading the HR function by developing HR strategy, contributing to organizational strategy, influencing people management practices, and monitoring risk."

Many HR associations and thought leaders—myself included—find it very difficult to obtain the pre-approved business credits for our planned programs.

Every five years, HRCI reviews and updates the content for the SPHR/SPHRi exams. Recently I had the privilege of serving as a subject matter expert (SME) at the SPHR/SPHRi Practice Analysis at HRCI headquarters in Alexandria, Virginia. This honor afforded me the opportunity to spend a week with HR executives and academics from around the world. The twelve of us represented the US, China, Russia, Mexico, Jamaica, Israel, and India.

Figure 1: Working hard with HRCI

During our week together, we discussed and debated the pre-requisites and accountabilities of our profession. We explored the skills and knowledge needed for HR professionals and shared our recommendations for exam content changes with the HRCI team.

This experience led me to a significant epiphany. When we were debating our content recommendations, I was campaigning for the exam content to assess a highly strategic skill set. However, my inputs were described as "aspirational" by others in the group. In response, I asked that we back up and define the profile of the typical SPHR certification holder. It was through this discussion that I realized I had been categorizing the SPHR as a distinction for a Strategic HR professional. I had come to this assumption based upon the criteria established for the awarding of business credits to recertification programs. Although the criteria for business credits can be considered strategic in nature, that is not the total scope of the SPHR. I was reminded that the certification was an acronym for Senior Professional in HR, not

Strategic Professional in HR. The content is designed to assess the skills and knowledge of an HR professional who has extensive experience but not necessarily a strategic perspective. I decided it was time to start a profession-wide dialogue to develop a common language and benchmark criteria for Strategic HR Leadership.

THE FIVE DISTINCTIONS OF A STRATEGIC HR LEADER

Since 2008, I have been planning and facilitating Strategic HR conferences across the US. I have delivered hundreds of keynote addresses on the subject of Strategic HR. And I have engaged in countless one-on-one conversations on this subject with business leaders. For over two years, I embarked on an informal research study that collected the broad perspectives of thousands of HR and business professionals. In every venue possible, I asked respondents to identify the distinctions that differentiate Strategic HR from Traditional/Transactional HR. I wanted to know how similar—or dissimilar—our perspectives were.

After collecting mountains of data, I realized that our collective opinion of what constitutes a strategic approach could be summarized in five distinct categories: Impact, Influence, Inspiration, Innovation, and Integration.

IMPACT: Strategic HR Leaders analyze data to predict and measure outcomes. We quantify the human capital ROI and our impact on business metrics.

INFLUENCE: Strategic HR Leaders are adept at developing key relationships with all stakeholders. Along with an expertise that awards credibility, these relationships ensure our acceptance as an integral contributor to organizational planning and leadership efforts.

INSPIRATION: Strategic HR Leaders are the ambassadors of organizational culture. We study neuroscience and apply psychological methodologies to ensure a work environment that fosters employee engagement and personal accountability.

INNOVATION: Strategic HR Leaders challenge convention, look to the future, and manage change. We utilize technology, social science principles, validated research findings, and changing market trends to deliver proactive HR strategies.

INTEGRATION: Strategic HR Leaders truly understand the business drivers and collaborate closely with our non-HR colleagues to deliver practical human capital solutions that are highly valued throughout the organization.

SEIZE THE DAY

According to Charles S. Jacobs, the author of *Management Rewired: Why Feedback Doesn't Work and Other Surprising Lessons from the Latest Brain Science*, if you want to implement systematic change, you must first get everyone's attention.

Humans resist change because our subconscious motivates us to maintain the status quo. Familiar circumstances trigger feelings of comfort, knowing, and security. To transcend resistance, people need to see that the rules of the game have changed drastically. The perception of a new reality disrupts the brain's automatic processing tendencies. We are, in essence, shocked into understanding that adapting is emotionally safer than resisting.

And, as you are keenly aware, we are currently experiencing shocking events on multiple levels. This new normal provides the perfect opportunity to institute major changes that may have been challenging in the past. This is the perfect time to seize the moment.

A few months back I attended a leadership development clinic. In order to explore our personal values, the facilitator asked us to identify a character in a film or book that we admire and can relate to. She wanted us to really think about how this character inspired us so that we could better understand ourselves. I immediately chose Mr. Keating (played by Robin Williams), the English teacher at Welton Academy in the cinematic marvel, *Dead Poets Society*.

This movie is probably older than most of you, so here is the gist of the story according to Wikipedia:

> In 1959, shy Todd Anderson attends high school at Welton Academy, an all-male, elite prep school. Neil Perry is his roommate and Todd quickly makes friends with Knox Overstreet, Richard Cameron, Stephen Meeks, Gerard Pitts, and Charlie Dalton.

> They are inspired by the unorthodox teaching methods of the new English teacher, John Keating, a Welton alumnus who encourages his students to "make your lives extraordinary," a sentiment he summarizes with the Latin expression carpe diem, meaning "seize the day." His methods attract the attention of strict headmaster Gale Nolan.

Upon learning that Keating was a member of the unsanctioned Dead Poets Society while he was at Welton, Neil restarts the club and he and his friends sneak off campus to a cave where they read poetry and verse. As the school year progresses, Keating's lessons and their involvement with the club encourage them to live their lives on their own terms.

Neil discovers his love of acting and gets the role of Puck in a local production of *A Midsummer Night's Dream*, despite the fact that his domineering father wants him in the Ivy League. Keating helps Todd come out of his shell and realize his potential when he takes him through an exercise in self-expression, resulting in his composing a poem spontaneously in front of the class.

I explained that Mr. Keating inspired me because I too sought to encourage others to think differently. I like to consider myself a thought leader, and Mr. Keating's unorthodox methods and willingness to challenge convention resonated with me. I could relate to his passion and desire to engage others in their journey toward a purposeful path in life. I declared that one of my greatest personal values is to make a difference.

I left the session with greater clarity, energized to continue to develop my newly proclaimed value. However, as I reflected on the movie, I remembered some of the darker scenes . . .

However, Charlie takes things too far when he publishes an article in the school newspaper in the club's name demanding that girls be admitted to Welton. The headmaster speaks with Keating, warning him that he should discourage his students from questioning authority.

Neil's father discovers his son's involvement in the play and forces him to quit on the eve of the opening performance. Defying his father, Neil continues. His father unexpectedly shows up at the performance. He takes Neil home and says he has been withdrawn from Welton, only to be enrolled in a military academy to prepare him for Harvard so he will become a doctor. Unable to find the courage to stand up to his father, and lacking any support from his concerned mother, a distraught Neil commits suicide.

In distress I contacted the clinic facilitator, Megan, and explained my turmoil. The fact that Mr. Keating discouraged conformity and asked his students to *carpe diem* had led to a tragedy.

I pondered how this related to my value of making a difference. Was I leading others down a destructive path? Is conventionalism really a better approach than progressive thinking? Was my message misguided? This may sound trite to you, but I was perplexed and concerned. I started to really question myself because another of my personal values is "Don't do any harm while trying to do good."

In her wisdom, Megan simply instructed me to think about it. So, I did the logical thing and actually watched the movie again for the first time in a decade or so. The ending was enlightening.

Keating is fired and the headmaster takes over teaching his class. Keating interrupts the class to gather his belongings. As he leaves, Todd stands up on his desk and quotes a line in a poem "O Captain! My Captain!", which prompts the other members of the Dead Poets Society to do the same.

I was moved by the lesson the boys took away from their experience. They had developed such an admiration for Mr. Keating and his unique style that they were willing to risk expulsion to show him the impact he had made. However, my real aha moment was what I realized about Mr. Keating.

As an alumnus of Welton Academy, he knew that his teaching style would be challenged, and yet he did it anyway. He knew that the school administration and the parents would disapprove, yet he did it anyway. He knew that his path forward would be difficult, yet he did it anyway. He knew he would likely get fired, but he did it anyway. Because he knew he needed to *make a difference.*

Although Mr. Keating is a fictional character, this movie inspired me to amend my greatest personal value: "I am called to make a difference, *accepting difficulty and risk as essential milestones on the journey."*

So for you, dear reader, I ask you to make a difference. Find ways to overcome your fears and hurdle the obstacles. Don't wait for a seat at some supposed table. This is the time to flex your gravitas and expedite your journey as a Strategic HR Leader.

Impact

Strategic HR Leaders analyze data to predict and measure outcomes. We quantify the human capital ROI and our impact on business metrics.

Value-Added HR

Value is an economic premise. Usually described in terms of currency, value is determined by the intersection of supply and demand. However, in HR we tend to define value in less concrete terms. So, let's look at this from a business perspective.

If you do not have access to your organization's financial reports, getting this information is job number one. You will never be truly strategic without understanding the financial implication of your strategies. However, if you do have access to this information you should focus on three predominant areas to determine real value.

Every financial report contains many lines and columns with varying complexities. For the purpose of determining value, we will focus on revenue (or funding, for nonprofits), expenses, and net income. Your company may have different terms for these calculations, but they are an integral part of all financial statements.

Net income, often referred to as "the bottom line" (or budget variance for nonprofits), is calculated by subtracting expenses from revenue. This data point is a critical value metric to ensure the financial health and sustainability of every organization. True Strategic HR Leaders carefully consider how we spend our currency—our time, effort, and energy. And we must quantify the implications of our work to the bottom line.

When I meet HR professionals across the country, I like to inquire about how they spend their precious currency. I ask them to list the top priorities that they have been working on during the last week. What activities have they given the most time, effort, and energy? In almost every case, their responses can be categorized into three main areas: administration, risk mitigation, and value-added activities.

Administrative priorities are those that are designed to keep the business running smoothly. These tasks support internal processes—things like payroll, audits, report generation, data storage and security, benefit administration, leave management, and so on. These activities are considered overhead (the cost of doing business). Therefore, the costs incurred are expenditures added to the expense column.

Risk mitigation refers to the activities designed to prevent loss. This includes employee health and safety, compliance measures, employee relations, documentation, investigations, records management, and so on. These activities are considered overhead as well.

The majority of priorities reported by the HR professionals

fall within these first two categories. This is why we historically have been dismissed as "just a cost center." I assure you this is not meant as a compliment.

As a profession, we spend the bulk of our currency on risk mitigation. We generally view our value as primarily protecting the organization from any undue harm (and the costs thus accrued). But when you look at the impact to the margin, you realize that this defensive mindset may not be where we add the most value.

Let's explore . . .

Imagine you are a coach in the NFL. In order to be successful in your job, you must implement a winning strategy that results in scoring more points—and therefore winning more games—than your opponents.

Your offensive plays must be effective at moving the ball down the field and into the end zone, while your defensive strategies must prevent your opponents from doing likewise.

If you, the coach, decide to invest the majority of your time, effort, and energy into building a strong defense, you're inevitably bound to neglect your offense. You will most likely be very successful at preventing the other teams from scoring, but how will your team score? Even if you're perfect at executing your mission, the best you can hope for is a 0-0 tie. Is that a winning strategy?

Value-added activities are those that increase the bottom line, either adding revenue or reducing expenses. In other words, they represent your offense.

Since the economic downturn in 2008, HR has been continually asked to do more with less. In many ways, we rose to the challenge! We have been incredibly successful at reducing expenses. But I fear that the bone may have been picked dry.

There may be some opportunities to cut minor costs, and we should remain vigilant. But I do not believe that we can establish ourselves as Strategic HR Leaders on the sole basis of identifying additional significant cost savings. On the contrary, we will likely see compensation continue to rise and double-digit increases for employer-based health insurance premiums.

In HR we are fond of saying that our employees are our greatest asset. It is a clever statement, and it makes us feel all warm and fuzzy. However, in business conversations, an asset is usually considered an owned entity than gains value through equity and can be liquidated or borrowed against to increase income. So, eyebrows tend to rise when we refer to our employees as assets. If you look closely at your financial statements (or variance reports for nonprofits), you will likely find that your employees, namely their wages and benefits, are among the organization's top expenses. But, stating that our employees are our greatest expense doesn't sound as clever.

So, look at it this way . . . our employees are our greatest *investment*.

Calculating the return on your investment (ROI) is a strategy used to ensure wise investments. It is customary to project the cost of an expenditure versus the value added over time.

For example, imagine that you are meeting with your personal financial advisor and she informs you of a lucrative investment opportunity. She asks you to write a check for $10,000 and she will add the stock shares to your retirement account. Your first question is likely "What is the return on my investment?" Your decision to invest should be based on the value of the ROI.

But what if she tells you that you will be paid $10,000 at the time of your retirement? Do you invest? No—that's a lousy investment with no ROI.

Calculating the ROI is a standard practice for analyzing major expenditures in all business areas except one. And it just happens to be the most expensive one: our employees. When was the last time you discussed your HR-ROI (the return on your human capital investments)? Probably never.

But you are most likely involved in designing a compensation structure, hiring and monitoring headcount, distributing pay increases, negotiating labor agreements and vendor contracts, setting a training budget, and many other functions that highly impact the financial statements. You may not realize it, but you have a great impact on your organization's human capital investments. So how do you increase the HR-ROI?

To move the HR-ROI dial, you must start by clearly defining success. Most HR professionals are well versed in evaluating individual performance, but do you know the key performance indicators for your organization?

Key performance indicators (KPIs) refer to a set of quantifiable measurements used to gauge a company's performance over a period of time. KPIs specifically help determine a company's strategic, financial, and operational achievements. In other words, the measure of success (or lack thereof).

If we are to improve our HR-ROI, we need to focus on performance that moves the KPI dials. Now, you cannot do that single-handedly. Your role is to ensure that your organization's *talent* is well positioned to drive improvement.

Because we have done such a great job of trimming our budget, we can spend the majority of our currency focusing on talent!

THE TALENT ECONOMY

When you break it down, talent is a moving target that has its own unique economy. Perceived talent is a prime driver of wage differentials. Most compensation structures are designed to assign higher wages to positions that require higher levels of skill and talent.

Compensation structures are generally adjusted based on wage market studies. The studies are published based upon research that has been conducted comparing the wages of similar jobs across a region. The studies usually report the mean, median, and range of collected wages. As wages increase in the localized market, organizations are wise to modify their wage scales to remain competitive. However, because companies are highly averse to reducing wages, the studies rarely, if ever, report a decrease in wages. In times of economic downturn, wage studies tend to report stagnant wages and reductions in workforce as opposed to decreased wages.

When we are reviewing applicants for hire, we analyze levels of talent throughout the process. When we have chosen the right candidate, we typically make a job offer that reflects a wage determined by the organization's compensation structure and the hiring team's view of the candidate's talent.

Historically, related job experience and subject matter knowledge have been recognized as the measure of talent. Therefore, individuals with vast experience in a related occupation or higher levels of education are more desirable and offered higher compensation. Individuals without related job experience or areas of study are either passed over or hired at a lower wage. This model often creates compression issues. As we are all keenly aware, a higher starting wage leads to consistently higher wages throughout an employee's tenure. In concert, an employee hired at a lower wage rarely closes the gap. Therefore, when the lower paid employee has acquired enough job experience, they will often resign and seek a higher wage elsewhere due to their increased perceived talent. And the system then feeds upon itself until wages are so highly inflated that companies need to prepare for wage warfare.

HR can truly attest to the battle scars of past talent wars. However, we typically are the designers of the compensation structures that handcuff us. We must look at this issue from a business perspective. Yes, we must remain competitive, but we must consider economic drivers beyond our inflated market studies.

First, we should consider the HR-ROI. If we hire employees at an elevated rate and demand 2 to 5 percent raises each year (to combat turnover and promote wage equity), we have elevated our labor budget and therefore need to exponentially increase revenue. However, every organization's goal is to consistently *increase* the bottom line. So, although our compensation structures may be effective at attracting and retaining talent, they can be detrimental to the company's financial success.

Second, we must realize that our perception of talent is flawed. If you believe in the premise of predictive analytics, you will see that a candidate's experience and education are not predictive of performance. Although beneficial for success on the job, not all employees with advanced experience and education are top performers. There is not a statistical correlation between experience, education, and talent.

When hiring for a specific position, it is best practice to screen for related job experience and advanced degrees and certifications. However, to identify predictors of high performance, you need to identify the common traits shared by those who consistently outperform their peers.

The ability to navigate complex and unprecedented situations is currently the leading predictor of individual success. No matter their title, top performers are adaptable, innovative, confident, and collaborative, and demonstrate a high level of personal leadership.

Therefore, to improve HR's impact, it would be beneficial to align our recruiting, hiring, compensation, training, recognition and reward, performance management, and coaching systems to reflect the greatest predictor of success: situational navigation.

CLEARLY CLEAR

In his book *The One Thing You Need to Know . . . About Great Managing, Great Leading, and Sustained Individual Success,* Marcus Buckingham states, "Effective leaders don't have to be passionate. They don't have to be charming. They don't have to be brilliant. They don't have to possess the common touch. They don't have to be great speakers. What they must be is clear."

Why is clarity so important? Four reasons.

1. YOU CAN'T WIN THE RACE IF YOU CAN'T FIND THE FINISH LINE.

Employees want to know what is expected of them and how they can excel. Many HR teams have put a lot of sweat and tears into developing comprehensive job descriptions to define just that. But take a look at your documents. Do they clearly define *success*?

Or do they (more likely) lay out the requirements for not getting fired? Because we are so hyper-focused on compliance, we have developed documents that are legally defensible (good job, by the way!), but they rarely provide a road map to excellence.

Since you already have a great legal document, you can stop worrying about the compliance demands. Now get hyper-focused on defining success. And—I am sorry—a document is not going to be enough. Clarifying success isn't that easy.

If your organization has clear, quantifiable, and relevant KPIs, congratulations—you are halfway there. If not, you need to work closely with your colleagues to establish them.

I recently started working with a company whose leaders felt they were clear about their definition of success. However, when I asked them to bring me up to speed, they literally sent me eight different documents. They were beautifully written pages with interesting graphics. Included among them were the five-year strategy, the ten competencies of a leader, the seven organizational values, the nine-tiered organizational chart, the ten-page compensation philosophy, and three other documents that I admittedly didn't read. Needless to say, I was confused. These documents did not relate to each other in any way. There were no specifics that I could pull out as a common defining message. Their intentions were good and they were on the right track, but they had achieved the opposite of clarity.

2. YOU CAN'T HERD CATS, EVEN IF THEY'RE TALENTED.

More appropriately, smart and highly responsible people will almost always strive to do the right thing. Sounds good. But their perspective of the right thing is understandably skewed by their specialized focus. We hire highly qualified employees so that we can trust their judgment and empower them to do their best work. Without a clear understanding of the broader purpose, responsible employees will choose a path that best meets the narrow needs directly in front of them. This is noble but misguided.

I worked with a manufacturing company recently to help improve the workplace culture. When I dug in, I realized that they had very complex technical KPIs that I eventually came to understand. However, the KPIs were very department specific. The sales reps would bid for jobs that were complex, with extensive specifications. In order to make the sale, they would quote a lower price than the competition. The operators worked hard to reconfigure the equipment to meet the new specs. The quality assurance team developed new processes to ensure the product met their rigorous standards. The procurement agent needed to order special supplies and the shipping team needed to update their software to package the product.

With the additional time and labor, the order failed to ship on time. Everyone was doing a good job and making decisions that met their separate objectives. But with all the added costs, the organizational margin was erased. We needed to align the objectives and establish KPIs that raised awareness of the interdependence of departments.

3. HOW DO YOU WIN IF YOU DON'T KEEP SCORE?

Highly motivated teams want to know how they are doing. They want to know if they are winning or losing. However, many organizations find it difficult to determine what constitutes success and how to achieve it. Yep, it's not always easy.

A few years ago, I worked with the Mall of America (MOA). They define success in terms of a great customer experience. If you are not familiar with it, MOA is more than just a mall. It boasts an indoor amusement park and an underwater aquarium and welcomes over forty million visitors every year. Delivering a great customer experience is fairly easy to accomplish. Visitors almost always leave happy and want to come back soon!

I also work with a healthcare facility. They too want to ensure a great customer experience. However, they do not have an amusement park or an aquarium. They also regularly perform colonoscopies and other invasive procedures. Their customers rarely leave happy and definitely do not want to return anytime soon. So, defining the great service was a bit more delicate for the clinic than for the mall.

For situations like this I have developed a framework in which to achieve performance clarity. The model consists of four intersecting outcomes: growth, efficiency, quality, and service.

I have found that these outcomes are universal. When you boil it down, every organization (public and private) shares these common objectives. However, like the Mall of America and the clinic, the metrics and achievement strategies can vary widely. It takes a lot of mental heavy lifting to reach the clarity needed.

So, I planned a leadership retreat for the clinic management team. We spent hours discussing the specifics of their outcomes. In the end we discovered a clarity that has measured and driven success for over two years and counting.

By the way, the service outcome was not that patients leave happier, but that they leave healthier.

During this process, I remind the teams that an outcome is the result we want to achieve. It is common for the discussion to get in the weeds and start to focus on tasks, strategies, and initiatives. We complete tasks, implement strategies, and plan initiatives in order to *achieve* growth, efficiency, quality, and service outcomes. But sometimes it can seem impossible to quantify these outcomes.

I also recently conducted a retreat with the senior management team of a city with a population of over forty thousand. Municipalities have many varied responsibilities, and it can be tempting to define success differently for the unique functions. However, this city was working on creating a unified team and breaking down the silos that had separated the organization for decades.

The solutions that came out of this exercise were as simple as they were elegant. After considerable refinement, the team agreed to the following outcome definitions:

- **Growth:** A continual increase in people who refer to our city as home. This outcome is measured through a metric that tracks residency, new business, sales tax revenues, school occupancy, and event attendance.
- **Efficiency:** We are trusted because we do our due diligence. This outcome is measured through anecdotal reports. The group tracks how often their decisions are strongly challenged by stakeholders.
- **Quality:** We set high standards for ourselves and often exceed them. This outcome is measured through self-reported personal accountability reviews.
- **Service:** We serve through strong relationships. This outcome is measured through internal and external satisfaction surveys. We are currently considering how to measure the quality of strategic community partnerships.

As we rolled this framework out to the organization, we had a plan to deliberately promote clarity. We knew that if this became just words on a plaque our time would have been wasted. We developed a deliberate communication plan. We wanted these ideas to be digestible. Every employee needed to understand and easily recall each outcome. If this framework became engrained in our culture, it would impact performance.

We made sure that each of the management team members was using common language and helping others relate the outcomes to the work they do every day. For now, we have only focused on the outcomes, but we will start to integrate the measures into our performance conversations soon. Stay tuned.

4. CLARITY IS IN THE EYE OF THE BEHOLDER.

When I am trying to discern the level of clarity on a team, I like to engage employees directly through what I refer to as point-of-view (POV) interviews. I find the greatest insight in how they answer two questions. The most important question I ask is "How do we define success?" And I follow that up with "How do we know if we are successful?"

These questions are so critical because they indicate the level of clarity employees have (or don't have).

Employees often respond, "Who do you mean by 'we'?" or "What is 'success'?" I always respond, "Whatever it means to you." Although they may become annoyed by my ambiguity, it is important that I do not project my definition of success upon them. I am looking for *their* understanding, which is an indicator of clarity.

Here are some typical responses from organizations that lack clarity.

"Success is getting our work done. Some days are harder than others. We are constantly being asked to do more with less. I come in early and I leave late almost every night."

"I don't know how much longer we can keep this up. Mary is looking for another job because she says her daycare is mad because she is late picking up her kids so often. Everyone wants to do a good job, but we can't seem to get ahead."

"My boss says I do a good job. I show up every day and I like my work. I have been here five years and I have never gotten a bad rating on my performance review."

"We have a lot of meetings about stuff. I am not sure what comes out of them, but I take notes and listen."

"My boss is constantly saying that we're not efficient. I'm not sure what she means . . . we're working extremely hard."

"My team is great; we get things done. Everybody here is really nice. But other departments complain about us a lot. They don't understand how hard it is to do our job."

On the flip side, here are some typical responses I hear from teams that focus on clarity . . .

"We have a set of organizational values. They told me about them in my first interview and I think people here genuinely follow them."

"Every quarter the CEO has a meeting to go over the financials with us. She lets us know when our customers are happy and when they're not. It is nice that she trusts us with that information."

"The company has metrics that are tied to our raises each year. If we don't succeed it is on us . . . all of us."

"My manager sits down with me regularly to talk about how things are going. We discuss my performance, the team, and how my work fits into the organizational vision."

"Our organizational mission is . . ."

"Our boss is a visionary. He is always talking about how we can improve. He believes in us and we know he has our back."

How would your employees answer these questions? You won't know until you ask. I encourage you to conduct your own POV interviews to periodically check for clarity.

INFLUENCE

Strategic HR Leaders are adept at developing key relationships with all stakeholders. Along with an expertise that awards credibility, these relationships ensure our acceptance as an integral contributor to organizational planning and leadership efforts.

LEADING THE LEADERS

A few years ago, as I was speaking to a large group of HR professionals, I stated that the role of HR includes *leading the leaders*. I was astonished by the pushback that ensued. Many in the group disagreed, stating that we needed to look to the leaders to define our focus and declare our direction. They even went so far as to suggest that we needed to be subservient to the leaders of our organizations. What I quickly realized is that their perspective was firmly grounded in traditional organizational structure and the chain of command.

Although we certainly need to align our efforts with the organizational strategy, it becomes exceedingly difficult to be a strategic partner when you are more focused on obedience than on partnering to drive successful outcomes.

So, I suggest that you may want to explore your beliefs about authority versus influence. If you believe that you need a bigger title on the organizational chart to be an effective leader, this differential is critical for your journey.

In a recent conversation with Kamy Scarlett, the CHRO at Best Buy, I asked if she had advice for those who are trying to gain influence with leaders in their organization. She stated with conviction that HR professionals need to understand the business. "Be a businessperson first," she said. When she joined Best Buy in 2014, she said she routinely asked her HR colleagues, "How were the sales yesterday?" She was conveying to her team that "in retail, the sales today determine the mood tomorrow."

A New Expertise

Each business leader offers uniquely relevant expertise that affords them credibility within the organization. In any organization, there are typically members of the strategic leadership team who specialize in technology. Others bring great financial acumen to the team. Operational leaders are adept at process improvement. The intellectual diversity of the team creates a collaborative environment that drives success.

Traditionally, colleagues would identify knowledge of employment law, benefits, payroll, and staffing as the expertise offered by HR. Throughout the 1980s, 1990s and early 2000s, company leaders were deeply concerned about minimizing liability and controlling labor costs. Therefore, HR was considered a valuable advisor.

However, that changed when the bottom fell out of the US economy in 2008. The rapid onset of the Great Recession caught many companies by surprise. Many leaders panicked and scurried to implement contingency plans. This drastic shift completely changed the priorities of most organizations. No longer were we focused on risk mitigation because lawsuits were, frankly, the least of the worries. Many HR professionals became entrenched in workforce reduction activities. And we often found our own names on the bottom of the pink slip list.

Companies were reduced to bare-bones survival strategies. Just keeping the lights on and the doors open was a challenge. Many necessary functions were outsourced in an effort to control administrative labor costs. This gave rise to the surge of Professional Employer Organizations (PEOs) that we see today. In the process, CFOs realized that these vendors could provide many administrative services faster and cheaper than in-house staff—including payroll, benefits administration, and compliance (and eventually staffing).

Needless to say, when the economy began to recover, HR professionals discovered that we were now living in a brand-new world. No longer were our traditional HR skills in high demand.

I believe we are experiencing a similar renaissance today. With the challenges we face in the era of COVID-19, organizational priorities and strategies seem to be changing by the hour. We are winging it as we go along.

COVID-19 has savaged the American economy in 2020. The Bureau of Labor Statistics confirmed the worst unemployment rate since 1933, and the US experienced a record 32.9 percent drop in GDP. Vaccine production is finally ramping up, yet widespread distribution still eludes us as we enter a new year. However, in spite of these challenges, I am hearing a growing number of stories of how HR is stepping up and taking on the unique role of comforter, counselor, teacher, crisis manager, and Chief Zoom Officer. No one asked us to do this; it was a natural progression.

So how can we turn these tough times into an opportunity? *Develop a relevant expertise.*

Our colleagues understand the heightened need for compassion and empathy right now. They are looking to HR to provide leadership during this crisis because we are the people experts. So, we need to figure out how to do that in the best way possible—and quickly.

Although you probably won't find it in your job description, I would like to encourage you to become a student of brain science and behavioral psychology.

BECAUSE THEY ARE NOT ROBOTS

In my HR career, I have worked with many leaders I hold in extremely high regard. Often, one of these professionals— whom I believe to be top notch in their field—almost melts under the pressure of being a manager. Although they are intelligent, dedicated, and revered professionals, they inevitably walk into my office one day and appear to be broken. Their hair is prematurely grey, their shoulders sag, their face is scrunched up in agony as they say to me, "What are we going to do with Bobby?" or "Please help me with Sue." These managers have mastered the technical and administrative components of their work, but managing employees requires an entirely different skill set.

This phenomenon has haunted and puzzled me for some

time. So, I began asking the attendees of my leadership development workshops the question: Why is it so hard to manage employees?

I heard many good answers, but the best was, "Because they are NOT robots."

I was awestruck by how profound this simple statement was. Robots are predictable. We can program them to behave as we desire. They arrive with an instruction manual that explains how they work. We are trained how to fix them when they break down. And, each one is similar—if not exactly identical—to the next. None of this is true of humans.

Wouldn't it be great if our employees came to work with a personal instruction manual (and a phone number so you could call the help desk . . . their mom?).

But employees are afflicted by the human condition. Robots are equipped with a complicated computer program, but humans operate an even more complex system: the brain. We are all driven by human nature, which can be unpredictable and confusing. Humans can often be a hot mess. So, as the people experts, we need to learn more about how our brain works at work.

When our brain senses danger, it triggers our adrenal system to release the hormones cortisol and adrenalin. This hormone cocktail physically and psychologically prepares us to either fight our enemies or flee from danger.

When our ancient ancestors lived in caves, the fight-or-flight response was essential to survival. Every day they faced many life-threatening situations. Every moment was spent ensuring the availability of an adequate food supply, protecting the tribe from enemy attacks, fighting off ravenous animals, and competing for a suitable mate. During this time, our ancestors' brains were smaller than that of modern-day humans. As we have evolved through the generations, our brains have expanded to allow for the onset of our complex intellectual functions such as reasoning, planning, and analysis. Due to the technology of MRIs, we now know that these capabilities are housed in our prefrontal cortex, which is responsible for the aptly named "executive" functions.

However, when we are in the throes of a threat response, our executive function becomes somewhat impaired. Our primal instincts kick in and our subconscious takes over. We become less capable of analyzing and assessing the true level of a threat. Therefore, all threats (great and small, real and perceived) trigger a similar physiological response.

For example, an employee who believes a coworker is sabotaging her efforts will have nearly the same adrenal response as a driver being carjacked at gunpoint.

Our brains are similar to our muscles; when we overdo it, we can pull a muscle, which requires rest and time to heal. When we experience prolonged periods of stress and anxiety, our executive capabilities are diminished. To remedy this, we need a period of recovery.

Many HR professionals focus on finding work-life balance to reduce employee stress. Especially now, it is nearly impossible to forge that balance. Often, we encourage employees to use their vacation time and instruct them not to check their email while they are gone. I wish this approach worked because it sounds great. However, for me, going even an hour without knowing what lies in my inbox causes me great stress and anxiety. Many professionals report that they do not use their vacation days because their work piles up while they are gone, which only increases their workload and stress when they return.

So, what can you do to promote recovery? Well, that is highly individualized. Every person needs to figure out their own methods of recharging. But there are four universal methods that you can utilize. (Actually, there are six, but encouraging sex and the use of mood-altering drugs are especially frowned upon in the workplace.)

1. Exposure to nature. I know that sounds weird, but it is intuitive. It is the reason we love our pets. It is the reason we covet the corner office with a view. Our brains are wired with the desire to interact with nature.

As a matter of fact, a Norwegian study identified that having plants in the workplace greatly reduced absenteeism and advanced psychological well-being. In *Biophilic Design: The Theory, Science and Practice of Bringing Buildings to Life* (Kellert, Heerwagen, and Mador, 2008), the authors reported:

- Neuropsychological symptoms were reduced by 23 percent when plants were present. Fatigue reduced the most—by 30 percent.
- Mucous membrane symptoms were reduced by 24 percent overall when plants were present. Cough decreased by 37 percent and dry throat by 25 percent.
- Dry or flushed skin was reduced by 23 percent with plants in the workspace.

2. Sensory response. There is a lot of emerging science on this subject. Researchers are discovering that certain patterns of music, specific colors, deliberate smells, and meditative activity can trigger strong brain recovery.

3. Exercise. Physical activity stimulates the release of endorphins, dopamine, norepinephrine, and serotonin. These neurotransmitters are linked to your mood and overall sense of well-being. For example, after a nice long bout of aerobic exercise, some people experience what's known as a "runner's high":

a feeling of euphoria coupled with reduced anxiety and a lessened ability to feel pain. (Maybe I am doing it wrong . . .)

4. Serving others. This is the best one. Humans have an innate desire to help one another. According to helpguide.org, "Volunteering helps counteract the effects of stress, anger, and anxiety. The social contact aspect of helping and working with others can have a profound effect on your overall psychological well-being. Nothing relieves stress better than a meaningful connection to another person."

Understanding Eddie

As a leader it is critical for you to understand that our subconscious has a voice. This is the little person who sits on our shoulder and looks out for our safety. I have named mine Eddie Haskell (if you are under the age of thirty, you may not get the joke, but believe me, that is funny).

Eddie's job is to prepare me for all possible dangers. He instructs me to be on the lookout and jumps into action when he senses an approaching threat.

Eddie likes stories. If he does not have all the information to complete the story, he will finish writing the tale himself. And Eddie does not work for Harlequin; Eddie idolizes Stephen King. Eddie will concoct stories of epic doom because his job is to prepare me to survive in the worst-of-the-worst-possible worst-case scenarios.

Let's explore this . . .

Pretend for a moment that you have just checked your email and there is a message from your boss. It states that she and her boss need to meet with you right away.

What are you feeling? What are you thinking?

More than likely, your Eddie is telling you that you are in trouble. You are probably racking your memory trying to figure out what you did wrong. I bet you are starting to think of all the ways that your boss has failed to provide you with what you need to perform (fight), or you are composing a list of the other companies in the area that could use your expertise (flight). Eddie is preparing you to survive the approaching tsunami.

I highly doubt that your Eddie said anything remotely close to "Get ready my friend, you are being promoted," or better yet, "You're finally getting that raise you deserve."

Why would he? Preparing us for the good things in life is not Eddie's job.

THE RABBIT HOLE OF LOGIC

Our logic-based management systems are established on the premise that employees will improve when told that noncompliance will result in punishment (up to and including termination).

It seems only logical that reprimanded employees will focus on improving their efforts. However, the converse is usually true. The threatened brain obsessively focuses on fighting or fleeing, which almost never results in improved performance.

I have a good friend who works for a large food manufacturing facility. The plant is located in a small Midwestern town that boasts of a labor force with a stellar work ethic. This particular employer has a strict no-fault attendance policy that follows the progressive discipline model.

My friend took his performance at work very seriously. For over five years he never missed a day of work. He often bragged about the time he worked a twelve-hour shift with an untreated broken foot. He was the ideal employee, earning the award for perfect attendance year after year . . .

And then he had children.

As all parents know, babies get sick, often. My friend (whose wife also worked outside of the home) quickly received a verbal warning for work absences. Soon after, his infant son was hospitalized for pneumonia and he was issued a written warning for missing another shift. He was told that the documentation of his offenses would be put in his permanent file. (This was corporate protocol.)

My friend has always prided himself on being a good employee. The thought of having a permanent reprimand in his file rocked him to the core. He instantly began to talk about finding a new job. His work suffered, and his coworkers told me that he was no longer very fun to be around.

This lasted for almost six months. And, although I am happy to report that my friend is still employed and performing well at the plant, he is keenly aware—eight years later—that the written warning remains in his record.

The other unfortunate side effect of this employer's attendance policy is that many of the workers learned early on how to "play the system." They keep a running count of their occurrences and manage the intervals between absences. After twelve months, an occurrence will drop off their record, and the employees feel free once again to miss a day at work.

Keep in mind these are the same employees that make up the town's labor force with the reputation of having an outstanding work ethic. These are not problem employees. Most of the staff considers the attendance policy to be an extension to their PTO (paid time off) benefits.

Earlier, I referenced the book *Management Rewired: Why Feedback Doesn't Work and Other Surprising Lessons from the Latest Brain Science* by Charles S. Jacobs. This is the best book I have read on the matter of applying brain science and psychology in the workplace. In the book, Jacobs suggests:

"Businesspeople are taught to make decisions with facts and logic and to avoid emotional bias. But according to the latest research, we almost never decide rationally, despite thinking that we do. Our experiences carry an emotional charge, encoded in the synapses of our neurons. And when we try to deny what our emotions tell us, we lose what we've learned from the past. That's just one of many recent discoveries that help explain why management is so challenging. Much of the conventional wisdom taught to managers is not only inadequate, it produces the opposite of what is intended. The better path is frequently counterintuitive.

"Once we understand the lessons of neuroscience, we can create more effective strategies, inspire people to maximize their potential, and overcome the biggest hurdle to improving business performance—making change stick."

If HR can develop an expertise based in neuroscience and proven psychological methodologies to enhance our other talent management tools, we will bring to the table a valued perspective that is in high demand. Most leaders pride themselves on their understanding of management techniques. However, their approach is generally based on logical principles that are ineffective and often have a negative impact on performance. If HR can apply this new expertise, I believe we will not only be viewed as a strategic partner, but we can also *lead the leaders.*

It's All about Relationships

Recently, as I was driving along the highway, a vehicle cut me off. My first instinct was to give the driver my famous one-finger wave, but I resisted because my kids were with me.

As my annoyance continued to simmer, we came to a stoplight. When I looked into the rearview mirror of my vehicular adversary, I didn't see the monster I'd expected to see. I recognized that it was my friend Jodi. Instantly I offered her the five-finger wave. I was so excited because I had not talked with her in a while. I thought, *I wonder if she sees me waving . . . I should call and invite her over for a cup of coffee. I hope she and her family are doing well.*

What changed? The relationship!

It was very easy for my Eddie to assume this driver had bad intentions because I had no information to the contrary. It is natural for our subconscious to assess the risk posed to us by others. But unfortunately, it is one of our worst instincts to see strangers as a threat.

> "Strong relationships grow when you stop projecting yourself onto someone else and start to see them for who they uniquely are."
> —Marcus Buckingham

Because of my preexisting relationship with Jodi, Eddie shut his big fat mouth. I could trust that her intentions were not malicious. Truly believing that her behavior was unintentional, my rage instantly gave way to harmony.

This is the magic of relationships.

In the workplace, relationships are often predetermined by function or geography. The essence of the work requires us to interact with others doing similar work in common spaces. However, transitioning from coworkers to teammates requires more.

How do you forge strong relationships?

Consider these three crucial elements: authenticity, vulnerability, and empathy.

AUTHENTICITY

Leaders have long been evaluated on their ability to lead with professionalism. Translated into business speak, this means that to be viewed as a strong leader you must conform to a set of ideals and leave your personality (and emotions) at the door.

However, in the last few years the concept of authentic leadership has gained momentum. Leadership is no longer an act of demanding respect. Leadership is now measured by a willingness of others to follow. Employees now want to know who their leaders really are. They need to understand what you value, what is important to you.

Best Buy's Kamy Scarlett says that strong leaders openly embrace "authenticity and passion," and she encourages all leaders to be vulnerable. She describes integrity as "bringing your entire self instead of trying to be someone you are not." She urges all of us to know that *you are enough.* Let's stop "should-ing" ourselves.

> "Being authentic means coming from a real place within. It is when our actions and words are congruent with our beliefs and values. It is being ourselves, not an imitation of what we think we should be or have been told we should be. There is no 'should' in authentic."
> —Diane Mottl, MSW

Discovering who you truly are is much more effective than trying to become the person you believe others want you to be.

Kamy describes courage, vulnerability, empathy and grace as the inclusive behaviors of leadership. She believes leaders need to give others permission to be imperfect. "If you show up as 'nailed it,' others believe they have to as well." For authenticity and trust to become embedded in the workplace culture, she says leaders need to demonstrate a willingness to be vulnerable.

I am often asked if trust is given or earned. This "Who goes first?" question is similar to the chicken-or-egg debate. For much of my career I made the argument that trust is given, not earned. My reasoning was embedded in the premise that if someone does not trust me, for whatever reason, it is their choice to change their impression of my trustworthiness. I can pay them a million dollars or tap dance all day. If their mind is set, there is nothing I can do to *earn* their trust.

I still believe this to be true, but I know this philosophy is no longer sufficient. I have spent a lot of sweat and tears coaching leaders about trust. Through this work I have come to the realization that the question is not about who goes first . . . it is about the relationship. Trust requires two persons willing to bring their authentic selves into a relationship of *shared* trust. Both must focus on giving and earning trust every day.

VULNERABILITY

Vulnerability is a natural instinct for most strong leaders. However, historically, those who showed their vulnerability in the workplace were considered weak. We often heard "You need to be tough to make it in this business." Or "Don't take it personally; it's just business." And "There's no crying in baseball."

"Owning our story and loving ourselves through that process is the bravest thing we'll ever do."
—Brené Brown

However, with the shift toward authentic leadership, leaders understand that when they allow themselves to be vulnerable relationships are strengthened. Giving a stage to your true thoughts, feelings, strengths, and shortcomings gives others the agency to be authentic and vulnerable as well. Which, by the way, is crucial for mental well-being.

I witnessed the virtues of vulnerability firsthand while working with a rural electrical cooperative. The newly named CEO (we'll call him Tom) was a sharp contrast to his more traditional predecessor. Prior to Tom's appointment, the organizational culture was analogous to a commonly held "command and control" philosophy. There was a strong adherence to the hierarchy and a chain of command. Whoever had superiority was in charge. All subordinates were expected to just do their job.

Similar to most electrical cooperatives, a real sense of machismo was prevalent. Young, strapping (usually male) linemen are tasked with climbing electrical poles to ensure service delivery to the co-op's members. After a typical midwestern ice storm, these determined employees put their own safety at risk to make the needed repairs to curtail a power outage.

The primary means of communication in this environment was sarcasm. There was a palpable division between the workers and management. And to further fuel the cultural divide, the corporate offices were in a separate location from the operational centers. Needless to say, "us versus them" silos were embedded deep within the company culture. Many employees were clearly in "what's in it for me?" mode. They showed up simply to earn a paycheck. With Tom's arrival, things slowly began to change. His philosophy was different: more collaborative, less hierarchical, highly purposeful, and customer driven.

Tom deliberately set out to forge a new culture. He would often say, "If a leader believes they're the smartest person in the room, they are probably wrong." He wanted every employee to feel empowered to take an active part in their mission: "Serving our members. Always."

But you are probably well aware that driving culture change is hard work! So, what was Tom's secret? Unbridled vulnerability. He did not set out to be a vulnerable leader; it just came naturally for him. He told me that he usually felt like a fish out of water. The energy sector is not known for its progressive leadership style. Command and control remain a rule of thumb.

But Tom is a strong believer that it can be different and should be different. He is passionate about people. He knows that the technical facets of the work are important, but he understands that the employees determine the collective success.

When I began working with Tom and his team, I appreciated his approach almost immediately. I realized he wears his passion on his sleeve. We developed a strategy to take the company from a "me" mindset to a "we" culture.

We laid out a plan to drive this new perspective. At an all-hands meeting, Tom stood up to launch the initiative. This was the first time most employees had heard anything about company culture. They were originally very uninterested. They just wanted to get back to work.

But as Tom continued to speak, I could feel the mood in the room start to change. Tom's core beliefs were evident. He shared the challenges he had experienced throughout his career. He spoke of past failures. He admitted to occasionally going along with things that he didn't think were right just to appease superiors. And then he got even more vulnerable.

As he laid out his vision, he began to choke up. He unapologetically shed real tears.

Now with a room full of linemen, I fully expected a level of discomfort that would send him reeling for composure. But instead . . . magic happened. The employees started to pay close attention. The sarcasm dried up and they were genuinely intrigued. He had their hearts. Who knew?

As our work progressed, Tom's vulnerable style continued. He developed truly genuine relationships throughout the company. He was not considered the boss . . . his self-proclaimed title was "Tom." Although we have had bumps and bruises along the way—and still do—the culture has observably shifted.

EMPATHY

Empathy is a powerful virtue. Unlike sympathy, which is an emotion you project onto someone, empathy is the keen ability to identify, understand, and relate to the emotions of others.

Without empathy, relationships are hollow. They become one-sided. They tend to erode into primary roles of taker and giver, which most of us have experienced at some point. It is exhausting to always be the giver. Strong relationships are balanced. They are rarely 50/50, but they should never be 0/100.

I recently had a front row seat to the profound impact of empathy in the workplace. A leader that I have been working with—let's call her Tracy—is an HR executive at a municipality. Throughout her career, she has held traditional roles, including recruiting, employee relations, and policy development.

Tracy asked me to join her on a journey to redefine her role. We began by discussing her strengths. It quickly became evident that Tracy has very strong relationships with many employees.

As you well know, employees tend to avoid HR like the plague. But Tracy has a unique ability to identify with, understand,

and relate to others. She meets employees where they are (literally and figuratively) and stands beside them on whatever path they may be embarking upon. The way they reach out to her is impressive, if not enviable.

Her empathetic nature not only makes her approachable, but it also enables her to coach others in a candid way without eroding their mutual trust. Even if she disagrees with you, you can be assured that she understands your perspective and has your interests at heart.

Recently, due to the loss of revenue during the pandemic, the municipality needed to furlough a few employees. Tracy's input to the process was invaluable because she foresaw the emotional impact on *all* employees. Her empathy enabled her to anticipate the response to the news. She advocated for comprehensive, compassionate communications. She wanted the employees to be as reassured as possible.

Since the onset of COVID-19, I have been making a concerted effort to reach out to my network. Staying in touch has always been difficult, but that's true now more than ever.

Before the country shut down, I was spending twice as many nights in hotel rooms as I was in my own bed. My office had wings and was fully staffed by courteous flight attendants.

I have business contacts from Florida to Washington and every state in between. Before each trip, I emailed a handful of folks and set up a time to meet for coffee or an adult beverage. In mid-March 2020, the world stopped. I was forced to cancel six trips that were on my calendar. However, as any extrovert will tell you, I have a deep need to hang out and spend endless hours solving the world's problems with like-minded colleagues. This, along with opportunities to speak to larger groups about my passion for HR, is the emotional fuel that keeps me going.

Lately I have been told countless stories about the limitations of Zoom and the isolation of remote work. It is hard to be resilient in a crisis without face-to-face interactions. When we *can* get together, we are required to wear masks, which hide the facial expressions we observe to read the emotions of others.

I just finished a Zoom call with a healthcare administrator I coach from time to time. She expressed that she was experiencing actual feelings of loss and grief in the new not-so-normal. For the past three years, her team has worked hard to create a collaborative culture. During the demands of this health crisis, they have fallen back into silos and usually only get together to share pertinent information or establish protocols. She misses the collaborative approach that had unified her team.

Relationships not only grant you *influence*, but they also give you *strength*.

DISTINCTION 3
INSPIRATION

Strategic HR Leaders are the ambassadors of organizational culture. We study neuroscience and apply psychological methodologies to ensure a work environment that fosters employee engagement and personal accountability.

THE ORIGINS OF "MANAGEMENT"

In the 1870s, French mining engineer and author Henri Fayol (1841-1925) refined his theory of management, which includes five primary managerial accountabilities: planning, organizing, commanding, coordinating, and controlling. This methodology is still widely accepted today as representing the cornerstones for organizational structuring.

In 1911, Frederick Winslow Taylor (1856-1915), published *The Principles of Scientific Management*. In this work, which was voted the most influential management book of the twentieth century by the Fellows of the Academy of Management, Taylor outlined the tools and methods for increasing efficiency in the workplace. Taylor was the first to promote the value of systematic observation and study of work in an industrialized economy.

The most notable of Taylor's assertions is that "management needs to provide detailed instruction and supervision of each worker in the performance of that worker's discrete task." This belief has framed the culture of almost every American workplace for well over a century.

Taylor's view of the worker was very distinct. Unapologetically, he surmised the typical worker to be unskilled, uneducated, and, frankly, stupid. His beliefs were somewhat rooted in historical fact. The average employee at that time had only an eighth-grade education. And most of the new labor class had grown up in an agriculture-based economy and possessed few industrial skills.

Taylor theorized there is no "skilled work." In manual operations there is only "work." All work can be analyzed the same way. In "The Rise of the Knowledge Society," an essay published in *The Wilson Quarterly* (Spring 1993), Peter Drucker wrote,

Highlights from Henri Fayol's Principles of Management

Authority & Responsibility – According to Henri Fayol, the accompanying power or authority gives the management the right to give orders to the subordinates.

Discipline – This principle is about obedience. It is often a part of the core values of a mission and vision in the form of good conduct and respectful interactions.

Unity of command – Every employee should receive orders from only one superior or behalf of the superior.

Unity of direction – Each group of organizational activities that have the same objective should be directed by one manager using one plan for achievement of one common goal.

Subordination of Individual Interest to General Interest – The interests of any one employee or group of employees should not take precedence over the interests of the organization as a whole.

"Darwin, Marx, and Freud make up the trinity often cited as the 'makers of the modern world.' Marx would be taken out and replaced by Taylor if there were any justice . . . For hundreds of years there had been no increase in the ability of workers to turn out goods or to move goods . . . When Taylor started propounding his principles, nine out of every 10 working people did manual work, making or moving things, whether in manufacturing, farming, mining, or transportation . . . By 2010 it [the manual labor workforce] will constitute no more than one-tenth . . . The Productivity Revolution has become a victim of its own success. From now on what matters is the productivity of nonmanual workers."

COMMAND AND CONTROL

Due to the influence of Taylorism and Fayolism, modern organizational design is deeply rooted in the following premise: Success will occur if the boss (who is in charge) makes the ultimate decisions of who, what, when, where, and how the work will be done; the boss incentivizes employees with the promise of rewards if they comply—and the threat of disciplinary actions if they don't.

This ideology is often referred to as command-and-control leadership. As in Taylor's era, this approach is effective when the work being done is highly rudimentary and repetitive in nature. However, in the modern workplace, this manual type of work is often automated or outsourced.

As Drucker suggests, the typical job today requires workers to excel at activities that require intellectual abilities such as scrutiny, diplomacy, adaptability, compromise, creativity, reasoning, conflict resolution, teamwork, perceptivity, speculation, and a host of other highly complex skills. This necessitates an environment that validates trust in the judgment of the players and awards enough autonomy to spearhead innovation. Unfortunately, the command-and-control approach restricts these abilities.

In a recent TED Talk, Daniel Pink, author of *Drive: The Surprising Truth About What Motivates Us*, surmised,

"What's alarming here is that our business operating system—think of the set of assumptions and protocols beneath our businesses, how we motivate people, how we apply our human resources—it's built entirely around these extrinsic motivators. For 21st-century jobs, this can result in huge losses of resources and hours of time wasted. If companies want to be efficient, they need to take a new approach. If we can get past this lazy, dangerous ideology of carrots and sticks, we can strengthen our businesses, we can solve a lot of problems, and maybe, maybe—we can change the world."

This hierarchical aspect is recognizable in almost every org chart. The concept of superiority, authority, and subordination is surprisingly still prevalent in the modern workplace. This perpetuates the misconception that employees will not perform well unless they are closely supervised. Therefore, there is a belief that leadership requires instituting rules and policies to assure compliance and micromanagement of staff to safeguard productivity.

Job descriptions, codes of conduct, performance improvement plans (PIPs), and the countless policies found in the employee handbook do nothing to describe (or instill) *great* performance. On the contrary, they detail the recipe to "not get fired."

We have conditioned our staff to mediocrity.

Progressive Discipline

Many companies have a progressive discipline policy. The underlying premise is to provide adequate feedback so struggling employees can modify their behavior and become compliant with the workplace rules and standards. The process often includes an incremental series of consequences: an initial verbal warning (which is usually documented in writing?!), a written warning, a PIP, a final warning, which may include a suspension commonly referred to as a "career decision day" (I have never understood the logic of suspending an employee—especially for an attendance issue—as it seems counterproductive), and finally, termination.

A PIP is a document given to the employee that clearly states the expected improvements. The employee is asked to develop a plan to achieve the improvements and a timeframe in which they must be realized. This approach seems noble and compassionate, but I think it is somewhat cruel. Unless a struggling employee is purposely sabotaging their own performance (in which case they will welcome termination), they have more than fully proven to be the least qualified person to determine how to improve their performance. So, you are simply giving them an additional opportunity to fail.

The career decision day is an unpaid day off for an employee to contemplate if they believe they can come back to work and be successful. The premise is designed to allow a problem employee the opportunity to resign as opposed to possibly being fired.

Although progressive discipline provides some legal cover for the employer, I have yet to witness a struggling employee suddenly become a superstar after receiving a warning or career decision day. Actually, because Eddie is actively involved, stress and anxiety often lead to poorer performance.

Progressive discipline can be useful when a decision has been made that the employee needs to go. Due to the clear documentation, the process can be the basis for an effective exit strategy. However, you should fast-track the incremental steps to minimize any negative impact on other team members.

Improving Poor Performance

If, rather than discipline, your goal is to turn around poor performance, what works? Well, I have utilized a couple of strategies that work well.

Dignity. Without the preservation of dignity, Eddie will *always* join the conversation. Many supervisors believe that giving employees constructive feedback about their failings will elicit better results. This isn't inspirational; it's judgmental.

Improvement lives in the future, not the past. Effective coaching conversations focus on finding solutions as opposed to dissecting mistakes and shortcomings.

Perseverance. A few years ago, my husband and I took our two boys to northern Minnesota for a weekend getaway. As I was checking us into the lodge, my husband came to me and said that the bag of snacks we had packed for the trip had come open and the contents were spilled all over the back seat of our vehicle. I quickly responded, "You should do something about that."

He smartly replied, "I am doing something about it. I'm telling you."

Although this was a sample of my hubby's cute sense of humor, the interaction reminded me of how workers often deal with adversity in their jobs every day. Too many employees have been taught that the best way to solve a problem is to send it up the chain of command.

I often see managers continuously running on the gerbil wheel, constantly scurrying to deal with this problem or that crisis. Managers are forever telling me about how their entire day was spent "fighting fires."

Dedicated managers are naturally driven to help others. They are instinctive problem solvers and are usually flattered when others approach them for advice. More often than not, the supervisor has a ready solution for most problems. However, the primary goal is to improve employee performance.

When faced with a problem, it is wise to facilitate the opportunities for employees to persevere and adapt (without putting them in a situation that could sink the ship). There will always be obstacles in the way of success. You can bet that behind every solution is another problem. The best employees are empowered to overcome the obstacles they face. They must learn to address adversity head-on and implement creative solutions to move closer to the goal.

This is not the most efficient strategy, but it is the most effective.

Natural Consequence. My kids think it's kinda cool that their mom is in HR. They believe that I spend my days hiring and firing employees. I repeatedly tell them that I do much more than that, but they are fixated. So, their response to a news story we heard on the car radio was not surprising . . .

The newscaster told the story of a mishap that had occurred the night before at a fast-food restaurant in New Jersey. The shift supervisor was conducting the store closing process and had removed the day's earnings from the till. A newly hired employee was finishing his shift in the drive-thru. After the doors were locked, the manager realized that the drive-thru worker had mistaken the bag containing the cash from the register for the bag of food prepared for the last drive-thru customer. OOPS.

My kids laughed. "Mom, you would have totally fired that guy, right?"

I had to think about that for a minute. Would I? Should I?

Humans are highly motivated by justice. We want to see bad acts held to account. So it makes sense that we would seek culpability for errors made in the workplace. However, provided these employees had made honest mistakes (and weren't willing participants in a caper), I would not fire or discipline either.

I have no doubt that the average employee in a situation such as this would be consumed with guilt and shame. Any disciplinary action would just add salt to the wound. There would be no other people on planet earth that I could hire who would be less likely to make this mistake again. The lessons learned by both employees is greater than the value of cash lost. That money can be allocated to the training budget.

Organizational Evolution

In his theory of evolution, Charles Darwin proposed that individuals in a population naturally have varying traits, some more suited to the environment than others, and that natural selection was the process through which organisms adapted. That is, the individuals with traits most suited to the environment would survive and reproduce, thus strengthening those traits in the overall population.

I believe the modern workplace can be compared to a living organism. The traits of an organization manifest in its work environment. Employees select (or don't select) employers based upon the attractiveness of the workplace and the organization's specific traits.

As a social scientist, I have an unyielding passion for learning about humans and their interactions. In my work as a business consultant, I have had the opportunity to observe and analyze many organizations. I have identified common paradigms as well as grave differences among companies in both the public and private sectors.

This work has led me to develop the Organizational Evolution Spectrum (OES). This model assesses the modernity of the workplace. Empirical research proves that workplace climate is a valid predictor of successful (or unsuccessful) business outcomes in the current knowledge economy.

Considering norms, ethos, and perceptions, the OES model characterizes the mode of individual organizations as either *surviving, striving,* or *thriving.* Keep in mind that organizations travel along this spectrum as a result of how they respond to changing demands in the workplace.

SURVIVING

The criteria to determine whether a group is *surviving* are fairly apparent. Leadership in this environment is very reactionary.

Accountabilities are focused on short-term gains or sometimes on just preventing a backslide. In this climate it is common for someone to hit the panic button and all are expected to shift accordingly.

Survival requires a strong sense of hierarchy to keep the gears turning. Managers are highly focused on GSD (getting stuff done). Employees are seldom asked for input and are often unsure of the mission beyond completing their long list of given tasks.

Needless to say, stress is continually elevated in this environment. The fight-or-flight instinct underlies most daily decisions and actions. A physiological cocktail of adrenaline and cortisol (stress hormones) all but eliminates the opportunity for fulfillment. Behind every Band-Aid solution is another gaping wound.

Although this reactive approach is occasionally necessary, it is not sustainable. This was glaringly apparent when I spoke with Gary (not his real name), the practice manager in a prominent ambulatory surgery center.

At the early onset of COVID-19, I reached out to check in with Gary. His team had shut down the clinic for two months in accordance with orders from the governor but had just reopened into the new not-so-normal. When asked about the strategy for success in the clinic, Gary responded, "Our goal right now is that no one dies." He was not joking. "All of the other stuff will have to wait. Right now, we are totally focused on infection control and employee health. If any staff contract the virus, we will be in dangerous, uncharted waters."

The sense of survival was palpable. Gary was completely overwhelmed, and the staff was incredibly anxious. But they needed to serve their patients, so they forged on. Their perseverance was honorable, but they sincerely hoped the crisis would soon pass.

This is a typical progression for organizations in survival mode—even when there is not a global pandemic. Sometimes, a heightened response is needed to stay afloat, but it soon becomes impossible to function with such urgency. This environment is ripe for burnout and is the perfect breeding ground for costly mistakes and turmoil among staff.

When leaders realize that a pivot is essential, they often begin a journey toward *striving*.

STRIVING

Organizations that are striving realize a strong need to improve. They recognize the value of strategic planning and employee input. They are determined to carve a path toward progress.

With great enthusiasm, striving organizations are quick to assemble committees charged with developing creative solutions to existing problems. Employees are encouraged to offer their opinions about the current state of affairs.

This approach is well-intentioned. Employees who believe that their opinions count are much more likely to be engaged. However, there are some drawbacks.

Randomly appointed committees are scarcely equipped to take a strategic approach toward problem-solving. They tend to gather and discuss the negative impact of the issue at length (often resembling a b*tch session), and are often perplexed about how to offer practical solutions. Without the appropriate expertise to analyze root cause, they ideate clever solutions that often prove ineffective.

Committee members usually gain a sense of pride when asked to participate but become quickly disillusioned because they fail to see real progress. I have witnessed countless committees that have disbanded even after just a short tenure. Or, even more detrimentally, the groups continued to meet regularly to cover meaningless agenda items.

When striving, organizations seem to be throwing an abundance of darts at a blank wall. There is no consensus on what constitutes a bullseye.

This approach is aimed in the right direction, but *thriving* organizations go quite a bit further.

THRIVING

Thriving organizations recognize that organizational evolution is not a foregone destination—it is a constant journey. Rapidly changing factors require these teams to constantly assess their progress on the Organizational Evolution Spectrum.

Let's take a deep dive into what it really means to be a thriving organization.

CHARACTERISTICS OF THRIVING ORGANIZATIONS

There are obviously many positive traits that contribute to the success of thriving organizations. However, in my experiences I have found several paradigms that are widely credited with being pivotal on the organizational evolution journey.

Thriving organizations are:
- Deliberate about culture,
- Focused on employee engagement, and
- Resilient.

THRIVING ORGANIZATIONS ARE DELIBERATE ABOUT CULTURE

You have more than likely heard the saying "Culture eats strategy for breakfast."

I have worked with many companies that have dedicated considerable time, effort, and resources toward the strategic planning process. However, as they implement their strategic initiatives, they often encounter numerous unforeseen roadblocks.

I was recently assisting a judicial district that covered nine separate county court teams to realize the strategic goals set out for them by the state judicial branch. Early on, one of the court administrators shared a story with me. He described the team's relentless efforts to develop a plan to drive the changes needed. He told me that the strategies were well thought out and executed accordingly but that they repeatedly faced challenges that they did not anticipate. They repeatedly returned to the drawing board to tweak the plan; however, they could not seem to gain the traction that they wanted to move the dial. He told me that it felt like they were running on a treadmill and getting nowhere.

He shared his epiphany that allowed the team to finally achieve some forward momentum. He described how the team realized that it was not the plan that needed to be tweaked; it was the culture. They realized that without setting the right culture as a foundation for the changes, their progress would continue to stall.

I can agree that culture eats strategy for breakfast all too often. But did you know *culture devours talent for lunch?*

I learned this lesson while working with a rurally headquartered company. They were notorious for setting audacious goals with the automatic assumption that they would be exceeded. Due to their remote location, establishing a firm leadership bench was difficult. They exhausted great resources recruiting competent managers. With every accepted job offer, rumors would spread of the latest superstar that would lead the team to great success. The new "golden child" would be just the boost they needed to blow the competition out of the water.

The problem was ... the unrealistically high expectations and toxic work environment quickly dampened their forecast. Often, the pressures to hit the ground running—and the negative work experiences—led to either the employee's failure and inevitable involuntary exit, or a quick voluntary departure to avoid the negative impact on their career.

This story is common to many organizations that are in surviving or striving mode. Conversely, I have found that thriving organizations are careful to clearly define their desired culture and deliberately foster its adoption. Then, and only then, can they see the fruits of their strategic labors and talent acquisitions.

Is there a best universal desired culture? Well, no, but there are some common workplace traits that prevail among thriving companies: common beliefs, putting people first, and purpose.

Common Beliefs

In striving organizations, leadership often thinks that workplace culture can—and should—be mandated. They typically dictate a set of corporate "values" and emphasize that individual behavior needs to be consistent with these stated values. Well-crafted value statements are typically posted throughout the building and detailed in the employee handbook. Although considering culture is a step in the right direction, thriving organizations understand that culture is a manifestation of common beliefs.

We know that human behavior is primarily driven by our subconscious, which is reflective of our true beliefs. However, most of the time we are not knowingly aware of what we honestly believe. The conscious brain can easily agree to behave in accordance with a set of prescribed values, but if one does not subconsciously believe in the intended spirit of the stated values, behavior will only rarely be in alignment.

For example, many companies realize that collaboration is key in the modern workplace. They understand that no one individual performs well without support and interaction with others, both inside and outside the organization. Therefore, the desired belief is "We win—or lose—as a team." This is not simply a description of behavior; this is a belief statement.

If employees think that they can be highly successful just showing up to work, keeping their heads down, simply doing their job, and not interacting with others, they clearly do not believe that "we win as a team." If one employee or department is rocking, but another is failing, how can we possibly win?

Imagine it like this . . . if you were in a lifeboat feverishly rowing, your clear definition of success would be to reach dry land as soon as possible. However, if you came upon others stranded in the water what would you do? Would you reach out and pull them in the boat or continue toward the shore alone?

If a customer receives bad service or a mistake is made, it is rarely the result of just one person's misstep. And unhappy customers don't just go onto Facebook and talk about Bobby the cashier's actions; they often report that the grocery store sucks.

To be considered a top performer, employees need to ensure that others on the team are succeeding as well. Then, and only then, can an individual be considered a rock star. However, if an employee does not *truly* believe that we win or lose as a team, they will continue to row toward shore by themselves while proclaiming, "It's not my fault; that is Bobby's job."

Thriving organizations understand this paradigm and intentionally focus on fostering a culture based upon a desired set of core common beliefs. Individuals are asked to embark on a journey to examine their beliefs through an organizational lens, while the role of the leaders is to facilitate each person's journey toward adoption. No one journey will resemble another. This process requires patience, as each person will forge ahead at a differing pace. However, leaders need to make it clear that refusing to embark on the journey is *not an option*.

People First

Many companies proudly proclaim a "people first" approach as a part of their employer brand. Sounds good, but what does that really mean?

When I work with such a company, I look for clear evidence to support that decisions are being made with *people* truly at the center of the equation. However, this is rarely the case. Most often, the converse is true. It tends to sound more like this hypothetical story:

Orders at Imagine Corp. have increased tenfold this quarter. With the approaching holiday season, everyone expects this trend to continue. Anticipating a ramp up, Barb, the production manager, realizes she will need additional staff.

Barb submits an official request to Tyler, the HR manager. Tyler approaches Rhonda, the CFO, to discuss adding an FTE. After the budget is adjusted for the new position, Barb is asked to develop a job description.

Barb declares a position title (operations supervisor) and works diligently to include all the anticipated necessary tasks in the comprehensive job description. Although this position won't supervise any workers, Barb knows that the title needs to be categorized at the supervisory level to garner the credibility and authority needed to complete the assigned tasks.

Upon receipt of the completed document, Tyler adds the obligatory "and all other duties as assigned" statement to the job description. He then carefully updates the organization chart to reflect the decision-making authority and reporting structure for the additional position.

After completing a market-based compensation analysis to determine the wage range, Tyler eagerly places an online recruiting ad that precisely describes the job accountabilities. Upon receiving several applications, he quickly eliminates those that do not claim the minimum required related experience and education.

Meanwhile, Barb is busy establishing a proper workspace for the operations manager. She works with Jill from IT to set up a computer with the necessary software and designates an email account. Barb knows that Tyler will spend the new hire's first day conducting the company's standard orientation, so she sets up a detailed training schedule for the remainder of the week.

At the weekly department meeting, Barb describes the new position to the team and dictates the work that will be reassigned. She instructs them to send all production reports to the new supervisor's email.

And after all the decisions surrounding this role are finalized, a person is hired to do the work. People first? Really?

This is more of a function-first approach, characterized by the *work* being centered as the foundation of the decision-making process. We wrap all subsequent decisions—duties, structure, wage ranges, training, team, metrics, technology, processes, structure, rules, hiring, accountabilities, and title— around the logical function of the job.

The chances are low that the decisions previously made will be the best match for the *human* that will actually be doing the work. Every person is unique with distinct strengths, work methods, learning and decision-making styles, support needs, aspirations, and personality characteristics.

Thriving organizations take a different approach. They put human nature and individualization at the center of all decisions. They wrap the function decisions around the people, thereby adopting a talent-centric approach.

I routinely meet professionals who are seeking the next step in their career. When I am approached by someone that I find particularly impressive, I willingly reach out to my network to recommend them. However, I am often given the response, "We do not have any openings right now. Tell her to send us her resume and we will keep it on file." What a missed opportunity!

Thriving organizations that adopt a talent-centric approach usually respond like this:

> "Thanks for thinking of our organization as a good match for her. We are always looking for impressive talent. Please have her reach out to me and I would be thrilled to a have a conversation with her about her career goals."

When the candidate is brought in for an introduction, after discussing the organization's vision and mission, the company representative will typically say something along these lines:

> "Now that you know more about us, let's talk about you. I would like to hear about your passions and aspirations. Please describe the work environment that best

suits you. In what areas do you feel that you can be most successful? If you join our team, how will you apply your unique strengths to justify your compensation?"

The talent-centric approach provides the opportunity to build a highly talented team without the limitations of FTE, organizational structures, and budget constraints. Remember, an additional FTE is a great opportunity to make an investment toward improved results. If someone is a cultural fit with the organization, it is beneficial to allow them the opportunity to earn their salary.

I am sure many of you are skeptical at this point. I have heard your same concerns from countless others. They explain to me, "Talent-centric sounds good, but we have a job to do and customers to serve. We need to focus on accomplishing the tasks at hand." Many also resist because they worry about exposing the company to additional legal and regulatory risks.

I get it. A talent-centric perspective does not minimize the importance of the functional aspects of work; it simply creates an optimal environment in which employees can achieve functional excellence.

Purpose

The mission of your organization is incredibly important, an absolutely critical component of a talent-centric approach.

Most humans are inspired to give their best when they are a part of something bigger than themselves. Therefore, a strong sense of purpose is a core component of a thriving culture.

In 2020, we heard a lot about essential workers. Millions of messages of gratitude and encouragement for our heroes have decked the windows of American homes over the past year. During this pandemic, nurses, doctors, police officers, firefighters, public works professionals, grocers, truck and delivery drivers, janitors, housekeepers, social service workers, sol-

> "Our people don't need to be told what to do; they want to be told why."
> —Marcus Buckingham

diers, and many countless others have willingly put their lives on the line every day to serve the greater good.

The sense of purpose for these folks is at an all-time high. They are tired and overworked, but they persevere. They are underpaid and overworked, but they did not get into these professions to get rich. Long ago they made a personal commitment to serve.

How would your organization benefit if all employees felt a similar noble sense of purpose? Although not everyone can literally be saving lives on the front line, all humans want to feel essential.

In thriving organizations, employees clearly see a connection between their everyday work and the team's mission. They are keenly aware that their efforts are directly aligned with aggregate success. They don't attach their personal worth to wages (which is rampant in surviving organizations); they measure their value in the impact they achieve.

So how can you foster a talent-centric approach? As I mentioned in the previous chapter, it starts with a deep understanding of human nature and behavioral psychology. Luckily, there are many experts who are currently conducting related workplace research and sharing evidence-based people strategies.

THRIVING ORGANIZATIONS ARE FOCUSED ON EMPLOYEE ENGAGEMENT

"Employee engagement" is a term first coined in the book *First, Break All the Rules* (Marcus Buckingham and Curt Coffman,

Gallup Press, 1999). The book outlines Gallup's research based on 80,000 managers in 400 companies and introduces the Q12, a twelve-question survey tool for measuring the link between employee opinions and productivity, profit, customer satisfaction, and rate of turnover.

Through the Q12, Buckingham, Coffman and Gallup tapped into predictive analytics before it was mainstream. For the past two decades, thousands of companies have utilized the Q12 survey to determine employees' degree of agreement on the twelve questions it contains. The content of the survey tool documents a point-in-time measure of how employees *feel* about work.

Over the past twenty years, human resource departments all over the world have been charged with the monumental task of improving employee engagement. Along the way we have learned some valuable lessons.

Lesson 1: Employee engagement is not the same as employee satisfaction.

Employee satisfaction is a measure of an employee's comfort with the status quo. Satisfied employees tend to be happy with their current circumstances and usually prefer that they do not change.

In stark contrast, Gallup states the following:

"Engaged employees are involved in and enthusiastic about their work. They are 100% psychologically committed to their role. They are thrilled at the challenge of their work every day. They are in a role that uses their talents; they know the scope of their job; and they are more likely to look for new and different ways of achieving the outcomes of their role."

Although employee satisfaction is often associated with

talent retention, engagement is proven to be predictive of many additional operational and financial business drivers.

Lesson 2: Engagement is not a measure of success; it is a strategy to achieve greater success.

Most successful organizations have an affinity for competition. They look for opportunities to evaluate themselves against other companies or against their own past achievements. They are driven to keep score, and they relish winning.

Employee engagement survey results are not scores meant to indicate success or failure. Survey results are simply point-in-time data. I often compare it to the response given to a child who feels ill. The first action of most adults is to place their hand on the child's forehead. This act does not diagnose the ailment. It does not treat the malady. And it surely doesn't make the child feel well. It simply provides information to help you develop a plan for what to do next.

Similarly, the survey results should not be used to judge success or failure. In doing so, you will risk tainting future surveys. Because humans like to win, if the results are treated like a score, managers will start managing to the survey. They will unknowingly steer employees to respond more favorably on subsequent surveys.

You may also run the risk of magnifying the silo effect if departments benchmark themselves against other teams within the organization.

When asked why we should care about engagement, Gallup claims the world's top-performing organizations understand that employee engagement is a force that drives business outcomes. Research shows that engaged employees are more productive employees. They are more profitable, more customer-focused, safer, and more likely to withstand temptations to leave the organization. In the best organizations, employee engagement transcends an isolated initiative—it is the way they do business. The best-performing companies know that developing an employee engagement strategy and linking it to achieving performance goals will help them win in the marketplace.

Engagement itself is not the goal. We can't increase our prices or gain new clients by touting our team's improved engagement survey scores. However, when the results are analyzed appropriately, surveys can help to develop a robust engagement strategy. If effective, this strategy will foster greater *feelings* of engagement. It is these *authentic emotional connections* to the work they do, the people they work with, and to the people they serve, that is predictive of an employee's improved performance.

Lesson 3: Engagement is in the eye of the beholder.

I am often asked to help HR teams develop an effective employee engagement strategy. While planning to conduct a survey, I always warn the team to resist the urge to clarify the intent of the survey questions. Many times, well-meaning HR staff and managers try to calibrate the understanding of the questions asked. This practice will only skew the survey responses.

If engagement is a *feeling*, it naturally lies in the eye of the beholder. Just as every human is unique, so are the interpretations of each question. Common understanding is not the objective; insight into the true organic emotional drivers of each employee is the prize.

This is why I consider the survey to be only one of many considerations when implementing an engagement strategy.

It is imperative to determine a way to honor and tap into the individuality of each employee.

Lesson 4: Strengths are monumental.

I work with many organizations that embrace competency-based talent development philosophies. In this strategy, each position is analyzed to determine an exhaustive set of ideal competencies that are deemed necessary to achieve success in each unique role.

For example, the competency list for an operations manager will most likely include strong aptitude for:

- Problem-solving
- Decision-making
- Innovation
- Forecasting
- Communication
- Strategic planning
- Detail orientation
- Process improvement
- Data collection
- Analytical thinking
- Fiscal responsibility
- Walking on water (kidding, not kidding)

In a competency-based system, every operations manager is evaluated on this exhaustive set of competencies. In the areas in which the manager does not excel (which is likely to be more than a few), we institute a development plan for the manager to work on his or her "areas of opportunity." And in a few months, we will again assess the competencies to check for any performance improvement (or, more likely, continued deficits).

Sound like fun? Not to me. And probably not to the operations manager.

This system continually highlights weaknesses, which enhances any employee's sense of failure and erodes their confidence. Focusing on strengths, on the other hand, allows for greater achievement stemming from a firm sense of accomplishment.

Conventional wisdom suggests that a manager's greatest responsibility is to focus on helping struggling employees to improve their areas of weakness. Although we don't want to neglect these employees, the converse is actually true. The greatest opportunities for growth are in areas that an employee shows to be a strength.

Quite often, managers tend to neglect employees who demonstrate mastery. The presumption is that these folks have maximized their abilities. This is also untrue.

I recently read about a study conducted at a reputable university. They wanted to test the theory that focusing on our innate strengths leads to greater achievement, so they rounded up a group of volunteers and tested their reading speed. They separated the group into three categories based on the results: the slower readers, the average readers, and the fast readers. The group then participated in extensive training and a speed-reading practicum, after which they were again tested. The slower group had a modest increase to their reading speed. The average group saw no change in their rate of reading. However, the group that had the best initial results saw a tremendous increase in their reading speed.

Here is how Marcus Buckingham defines strengths:

"A strength is not what you are good at, and a weakness is not what you are bad at. A strength is an activity that strengthens you. It draws you in, it makes time fly by while you're doing it, and it makes you feel strong. And if you define a strength that way then the person best qualified to determine your strengths is you. You are the authority on which activities you lean into. You are the authority on which activities make you feel energized. Somebody else can judge your performance, or the quality and quantity of your work—but you, and you alone, can recognize your strengths."

Many top performing employees believe that they should dive in and do whatever needs to be done. This strong sense of responsibility is a part of what makes them a top performer. However, thriving companies encourage employees to not just dive in, but discover and leverage their unique strengths most of the time. This strengths-based approach doesn't just elevate engagement; it leads to improved performance.

I have witnessed many HR professionals implement initiatives designed to promote work-life balance and reduce workloads to prevent burnout. But many of these strategies are misguided. In the modern workplace work-life infusion is more desirable, and burnout most often occurs when a strength is being squashed or a weakness is being highlighted.

In the organizational development space, there are many professional assessment tools. From MBTI to DISC, most of these assessments are designed to categorize personality. Participants are issued a report that puts them into one of several boxes and describes their associated behaviors. These can be effective tools and I occasionally use them, but most often I utilize the Clifton

> Gallup reports that an average of 32% of employees are engaged, 54% are simply not engaged, but 14% are actively disengaged.

StrengthsFinder®, a program developed by Gallup (under the leadership of Don Clifton) to help people identify their innate talents and develop them into strengths. The tool uncovers your unique rank order of thirty-four Strengths themes. Your Strengths themes explain the ways you most naturally think, feel, and behave.

The StrengthsFinder is my favorite assessment for several reasons:

- It's more affordable than other tools and is therefore widely available. You can purchase the assessment on the Gallup website for a reasonable price.
- First introduced in 2000, it has stood the test of time and remains popular twenty years later. I recently talked with a client to whom I introduced the StrengthsFinder nine years ago. After all this time, they still use the assessment as an integral part of their talent development program.
- It is derived from Carl Jung's theories of personality and can be used in tandem with the MBTI.
- The thirty-four themes are appropriately named and create a common language in which to discuss our talents. When I share that my top theme is Ideation, those who are familiar with the tool understand that I am fascinated with ideas and novelties. Without further explanation they become aware that I have a talent for brainstorming.
- Most importantly, the StrengthsFinder does not put respondents in a category; it actually provides a unique profile of their top Strengths themes. Every person has all thirty-four themes, but they are ordered by prevalence. Gallup initially reports the top five

themes of each respondent. If you do the math, there are over three million possible combinations of a top five profile, but when you consider the unique analysis of all thirty-four themes, there is likely no other human being on planet earth with the same complete profile as you.

I often tell clients that if they meet a person with the same top five themes of talent, they should run out immediately and purchase a lottery ticket. I have probably reviewed over 5,000 profiles in my career and I have never found a profile identical to mine. I did meet a gentleman who shared the same top four with me. (I bought a lottery ticket and did not win, so that advice must only work when you match all five themes.)

When defining a strengths-based approach, you should consider two important areas of the Q12. Q3 asks, "At work, do you have the opportunity to do what you do best every day?" And the final question on the survey asks, "In the last year, have you had opportunities to learn and grow?"

The intersection of these two questions has led me to a monumental realization. I believe that our organizational structures do more to disengage our teams than any other consideration.

I know I am preaching to the choir when I assert that training and development plans should be a significant part of any engagement strategy. However, I have found that traditional methods greatly miss the mark.

To truly offer strengths-based opportunities to learn and grow, we need to throw out our dependence upon the organizational chart. This functional-centric tool only offers a singular career path *up* the organizational ladder.

The typical org chart manifests in a hierarchical culture that rewards being *above* or *over* others. To advance, employees must first excel in a lone functional area and wait for someone to die—or retire—to seek a promotion, at which point they must then compete with all their teammates to be tapped for a rare opportunity to learn and grow. This next step on the ladder usually entails the supervision of technicians. Beyond that, advancement consists of a series of mid-management roles which entail supervising supervisors. And to reach the top of the chart, one must be lucky enough to be chosen among the very few who are dubbed as an executive with significant strategic abilities.

Through my research and practical experience, I have discovered that this approach is highly limiting and essentially counterproductive. I have met numerous managers and executives who are passionate about the functional subject matter but don't really enjoy managing people. And I have met many frontline employees who aren't necessarily master technicians, but because they are driven to help others succeed, they would be great coaches if given the chance . . . or they may have true strategic capabilities that go unnoticed because they don't work in the C-suite.

Most organizations covet a balanced staff of skilled practitioners, strong coaches, and passionate strategists. Every person has capabilities in each of these roles. However, I have come to realize that each of us has a primary, a secondary, and a tertiary area of talent that directly aligns with our individual strengths.

My top themes of talent are Ideation, Strategic, Futuristic, Activator, and Communication. My strengths clearly align with my primary area of talent as a Strategist. My secondary area of talent is Coach, and lastly, Practitioner. In my career, I have often been disengaged because my strategic talents went underutilized and my inherent lack of detail orientation limited my opportunities as a practitioner.

Thriving organizations clearly understand that the realities of traditional organizational structures sharply restrict the application of individual strengths and greatly limit opportunities to learn and grow. Many organizations have instilled a flattened org chart as an effective engagement strategy.

Others have instituted a career "lattice" to replace the traditional ladder. This approach allows for cross-functional learning and growth, alternate advancement opportunities within primary areas of talent, and individualized career paths.

Lesson 5: The manager is key.

It is commonly held knowledge that the direct manager has a significant impact on employee engagement. Many studies cite that the quality of the relationship with one's manager poses the greatest likelihood of engagement—or disengagement.

Q5 asks, "Does your supervisor, or someone at work, seem to care about you as a person?" If you are a manager, this is an especially important question to ponder.

A few years ago, I met Tammy, the director of nursing at a small hospital. She was having difficulty connecting with her staff, and they were bleeding nurses (sorry-not sorry for the pun). She had worked in the facility for over twenty-five years, as had many on her team. When I was talking with the employees to gain insights into their team dynamic, most had a similar perspective. They told me that when Tammy was their coworker, she was friendly and helpful. They had all enjoyed working alongside her for many years. But when she was promoted, she changed. They shared how she quickly became cold and hard-nosed. They described her style as "overbearing" and they stopped relying on her expertise. It was clear the engagement of the team had dropped considerably since Tammy's promotion.

Tammy's story is not uncommon. Many new managers believe that a promotion requires them to change how they behave at work. I am sure most managers have been repeatedly told by well-meaning mentors and HR reps that if they want to be a successful manager, they can no longer be friends with their employees.

When I ask new managers why they believe they need to distance themselves from the employees I usually hear, "Because I may need to fire one someday." And although this is a true statement, the more accurate assessment is that you will probably need to fire a handful of people during your career. However, the multitudes of employees that you *won't* have to let go will greatly benefit from a meaningful relationship with you.

Most managers believe that giving feedback is the best way to help employees improve. But the truth is nobody really wants *feedback*; employees crave *attention*. Specifically, *positive* attention.

It is advisable for managers to check in with each employee at least once a week. I know this sounds overwhelming, especially in larger teams. But it can be as quick as five minutes. It is not the duration, but the frequency and sincerity of the conversations that matter most. Marcus Buckingham suggests keeping it simple and start with the question "What are you working on this week and how can I help?" And then they should just listen. It is important to resist the urge to make suggestions, point out problems, or get stuck in the weeds of past issues. Regular one-on-one conversations focused on near-term work are proven to forge relationships that drive engagement and, therefore, performance.

Lesson 6: Q10 is tricky.

The tenth question of the Q12—"Do you have a best friend at work?"—has always been controversial. Many companies have had difficulty digesting the idea of friendships at work, especially a best friend. I have talked with people who, for whatever reason, are actually offended by the question.

When asked about the best friend question, Gallup responded:

> "Gallup research indicates that friendships are vital to happiness, achievement and engagement. If you have a best friend at work, you are significantly more likely to engage your fellow team members, partners and internal customers. You are more likely to get more done in less time, have fun on the job, have a safe work environment with fewer accidents, innovate and share ideas, feel informed and know that your opinions count, and have an opportunity to focus on your strengths each day. Without a best friend at work, the chances of you being engaged in your job are one in 12.

> "Gallup tried wording this item in different ways, such as replacing the word 'best' with 'close' or 'good.' But the research showed that no other wording variations worked as well as 'best friend.' Gallup tested this item—and all items—using different wording to determine which words correlated best with positive answers from high-performing teams. Repeatedly, Gallup found that many people on highly productive teams answered this item favorably when using the wording 'I have a best friend at work.' On the other hand, Gallup found that people on teams with average productivity answered this item less favorably. Gallup's research shows that the 'best friend'

item has strong linkages to creativity, client/partnership metrics, and financial responsibility."

In many workshops, I have been challenged to justify the best friend question. I respond by asking the participants to share what they think about when they hear the term best friend. I hear things like joy, trust, fun, confidante, vacations, memories, laughter. One woman even said *shopping!*

I then ask them to tell me how many hours they spent at work in the past week. I usually hear between forty and sixty hours. Next, I ask how many hours they spent with their best friend from outside of work during that week. Most of the time it is zero.

I proceed to explain that dopamine, endorphins, and serotonin are called the joy hormones. When released in the brain, this adrenal cocktail has a positive impact on one's mood. I share how this influx of positivity can actually have a physiological healing effect and is proven to enhance cognitive abilities. Participants usually understand how all of the thoughts they had shared about a best friend would surely trigger this response.

Then I hit them with my point. If spending time with a best friend elicits joy and improves cognition, how different would your life be if you could spend forty to sixty hours a week with your best friend instead of zero hours?

I usually go on to share my personal story about why Q10 really resonates with me.

I first met "Amy" when I interviewed for a position with a large corporation in Minnesota. After being hired as a senior HR manager, I spent the first few months providing leadership development and upgrading the performance management program. I was soon asked by the CEO to partner with Amy to develop and facilitate an employee engagement training program for every supervisor and manager in the company—all 1,200 of them.

For the next four months, Amy and I collaborated to develop a two-day training program to deliver to the organization. During this time, I came to realize how much I admired Amy. Although our professional relationship introduced me to a new wealth of knowledge and techniques, it was our evolving friendship that encouraged me to explore strengths that I did not know I had.

Amy's confidence in me heavily outweighed that which I had in myself. Her energy level and humorous outlook made the work feel like playtime. Business travel was not the drudgery it had once been. I looked forward to our trips together. Although we always worked extremely hard, it felt like we were being paid to go on vacation together.

We brought diverse talents to the project, but our personalities meshed graciously. This partnership was void of the judgment, resentment, and competition I had experienced on many other projects. I never found myself questioning Amy's motives; I knew she had my back . . . and I had hers. We performed much better as a team than we could have as individuals.

We accomplished things that we never imagined we were capable of (including training all 1,200 managers two months ahead of our goal). We received a great deal of praise and accolades for our work.

It was through this experience that I realized the unlikely magic of having a BFF@work. I soon realized that lightning could strike twice.

Our company was searching for a new HR expert to head up the compensation and benefits department. One of our coworkers suggested that we interview her mother, who resided in Texas.

As soon as I met "Kate," I knew that she was overqualified for the job, but luckily we hired her anyway.

Kate was in the later years of her career and looking forward to retirement, but she fit in with our team wonderfully. She was a self-proclaimed Southern Diva, and I loved her outlook on life. She was proud and humble at the same time. She was confident and helpful all at once. And she may not have realized it, but Amy and I came to consider her our mentor.

Through her amazing ability to tell stories and relate her experiences to current situations, Kate provided profound advice to both Amy and me. She even taught us about the proper shoe choice of a true Southern belle. (I can tell you that bright color, a four-inch heel, and an abundance of bling are crucial.)

We quickly became the three BFFs@work. This relationship helped each of us achieve heights of performance that we could not have accomplished without each other.

Although Kate has since retired and Amy has moved on to a lucrative career with an international training company, their friendship will continue to have an indelible impact on me as a professional woman (and diva wannabe).

It's okay if you just can't stomach the best friend question. Simply understanding the concept behind the question can be incredibly powerful.

I am fascinated by employees who outwardly appear to love their work. When I meet such a person, I try to engage in a conversation to learn why.

On a business trip to South Carolina, I stopped for lunch at Boston Market. The very second that I walked through the door

I was greeted by a gentleman from behind the counter. He acknowledged me (from quite a distance) and shouted, "Welcome to Boston Market!" As I approached, I saw his name tag: Sam. Sam was an interesting fellow. He had a large neck tattoo, green hair, and multiple piercings. But this did not distract from his infectious smile. He eagerly took my order and directed me to sit at the table with the best view of the neighboring park. As he brought my order to the table, I asked him why he seemed so happy. He responded, "Because I love this job." When probed further, he told me, "My boss and my team have my back. We truly care about each other." As I finished my meal and walked toward the door, Sam looked up from his work to cheerfully thank me for stopping by.

Although Sam was definitely a unique guy, I have had similar conversations with employees all over the country. On another trip, I encountered a flight attendant who had turned the safety announcements into a standup comedy routine. When I inquired about his engagement, he smiled and informed me the primary reason is that the crew "has his back."

Lesson 7: Recognition is elusive.

I have facilitated numerous employee engagement surveys in my career. Almost all of them have a question that inquires if employees feel praised and recognized when they perform quality work. I have dubbed this the tanker question. Because on 99% of the surveys I have compiled, it receives the lowest scores.

A few years ago, I was invited to consult with a business services company that was concerned about the results from their recent employee satisfaction survey. They had spent the last twelve months (and a considerable amount of money) implementing what they considered to be a robust praise and recognition program. They had hosted many parties and conducted numerous prize drawings. However, they still *tanked* on the praise and recognition section of their survey.

Similarly, I met an HR executive who had made a commitment to visit every employee's workstation on Friday at 2 p.m. to pat each person on the back and thank them for the work they do. After a few short weeks, the break room became very crowded around 2 p.m. A few individuals remained at their desks because they treasured the attention from their boss. However, many of the folks who were found congregating in the lunchroom expressed their annoyance at the executive's insincerity. They made comments like "He has no idea what I do, so why does he waste my time by coming by to thank me each week?"

Early in my career, I worked for an organization that had about thirty-five corporate human resource personnel. To express appreciation to our employees, every month our department would host Friday Food Day. (I am not sure why most of these events tend to happen on Fridays, but they do.)

Keep in mind I am what you might call a "foodie." (I love food—especially the free kind.) I would ensure that I was in the office for every Friday Food Day. Please don't misunderstand; this was not your typical potluck that every office randomly has. Friday Food Day was a revolving array of delicacies and Grandma's best recipes. In the morning you could find egg bakes, assorted fruit drinks, and donuts glazed with maple frosting and sprinkles. Later in the morning you could waltz over to the Friday Food table and find popcorn, pretzels, and other snacks of all variations. By lunchtime, the table was filled with chicken wings, sub sandwiches, pizzas with all different toppings, and every casserole (aka hotdish for the readers in

Minnesota) imaginable. And by afternoon, out would come the brownies, cookies, and bars. It was pure heaven!!!

But on Friday Food Day, if I had been asked if I felt "praised and recognized for doing good work," I would have had to truthfully answer, "No more than any other day." I looked forward to every Friday Food Day, and I did not want this tradition to end, but it was not a direct response to my contributions. It was fun, but it did nothing to make me feel more appreciated.

Although I highly encourage every company to plan parties and food days, I must caution you against believing that these events are good ways to praise and recognize your team members. To inspire engagement, praise and recognition must be tied to actual performance in a meaningful way.

Too often I encounter employees who deflect gestures of appreciation. Somewhere along the way they were told to be humble, and that feeling proud of oneself is arrogant. As a result, any positive recognition feels undeserved or self-indulgent.

Recently I attended the funeral of my husband's Great Aunt Margaret. At Catholic funerals in Minnesota, we have a tradition in which all mourners gather in the fellowship hall after the interment to enjoy a meal prepared by the lovely volunteer church ladies. We were all sad, but Marge had lived a full life. I let out a snorting laugh when Uncle Joe told the story of how Aunt Marge had received a speeding ticket on her way to church at the ripe age of ninety-nine.

If you have ever attended a similar event, you are familiar with the wonderment of funeral cake. Funeral cake is not a flavor; it is the name for a plate of assorted individual pieces of cake assembled from an array of cakes baked by volunteers. A funeral cake plate is placed in the center of each table in the fellowship hall.

I look forward to the social support provided at this meal, but I also greatly look forward to choosing my piece of funeral cake. I usually gravitate to chocolate, but by the time I took my seat on this day, all of the chocolate pieces had been claimed by others. In concession, I opted for a piece of lemon cake. I have never really been fond of lemon-flavored anything, but this cake looked appealing.

After completing the meal of ham, German potato salad (a tradition in our town founded by German immigrants), and the obligatory whipped green Jello fluff with marshmallows, I tasted the lemon cake. OMG, it was delicious. It was so good that I was compelled to seek out and compliment the baker. One of the church ladies informed me that Lena had brought the lemon cake. I approached Lena and told her how much I had enjoyed her baking.

Lena immediately waved away my gratitude. She told me that she was not pleased with the frosting on this batch. She suggested I talk to Debbie because she had a recipe that was better than hers. I immediately flipped from impressed to confused. I began doubting my own ability to critique lemon cakes. I returned to my seat deflated and vowed to stick to my chocolate cake default.

So, what is the point of my story? It does not matter how much time or money you throw at employee recognition initiatives; if employees aren't prepared to accept the praise and recognition, your efforts are futile.

Job number one is to forge a culture that provides psychological safety for individuals to take pride in their strengths, own their successes, and accept appreciation from others. This is much easier said than done.

Not to make this a gender issue, but I often find that

professional women in their forties to sixties are especially prone to deflecting any gestures of recognition. We have been socially programmed since kindergarten to be humble and stay out of the limelight. This is noble, but it limits our performance.

Success begets success. Humans who feel accomplished accomplish more. Taking pride in your best work is not boastful; it is a responsible thing to do. As a leader, if you want to fuel inspiration, coach employees to identify, claim, and own their "lemon cake."

For each of us, there is a sensation that I call the rockstar feeling. It is the extreme pride and sense of accomplishment we feel when we win, complete a difficult project, solve a problem, or perform beyond expectations. It is a sensation like no other, and it motivates us to keep improving.

Although we can surely generate the rockstar feeling for ourselves, it can be magnified (and validated) by external feedback. However, the preferred form of feedback is highly personal. As a leader, you need to discover the fuel that lights each person's rockstar fire. And this is not an easy task. None of the strategies described in "101 Best Ways to Praise Employees" will be effective with everyone.

Whereas one employee may be totally energized by a customer compliment, another may be embarrassed by it. One person may relish being employee of the month, while another may be annoyed by it. (Don't get me started on the pitfalls of an employee of the month program. At best you are recognizing only twelve employees per year—and the likelihood of this approach being effective and meaningful to each is extremely low.)

If you sit down and have a conversation with employees to ask the question "How do you prefer to be praised and recognized?"

most employees will tell you that they would enjoy receiving gifts or a raise in pay.

But, I have yet to see the awarding of a gift card (even from the best restaurants) light anyone's rockstar fire. I have found that for most people, the trigger is often obscure and unanticipated, and is discovered only after great reflection.

For me, I often find myself experiencing a rockstar moment when I am speaking to a group. When someone in the room slightly smiles at me while nodding their head in agreement with what I am saying, I become essentially transformed into my rockstar self. I feel as though this person has stood up and declared me to be the "smartest person on planet earth." I interpret the head nods to be a direct attempt to tell me, "You are the brightest, funniest, and most thought-provoking speaker I have ever heard." And not only does my head swell a bit, but I also actually perform better. The continued fueling of my rockstar fire reminds me that I was born to do this work and I cannot wait to do it again.

Lesson 8: Engagement is only half of the equation.

I first heard Cy Wakeman speak at a SHRM conference a few years ago. I was immediately impressed when she announced she has eight (yes, eight) sons. She is a licensed psychologist, a former healthcare executive, and a best-selling author. Since then, I have had the honor to work with Cy on a few projects. My admiration for her insights continues to grow. Cy helped me understand that employee engagement is critically important, but it is only the beginning of a successful strategy.

In the 1990s, thought leaders were pushing the merits of high-performing teams. The strategy theorized that business results greatly improve when employees are held accountable by their peers. Companies across all industries began facilitating trainings about how to give constructive feedback to others. Many believed that this culture of freewheeling feedback would increase accountability and boost performance. But they soon realized they did not get high performance; they got toxicity. Employees were literally pointing fingers of blame and shame at each other under the cover of "I am just giving you feedback" or "I need to hold you accountable."

With the publication of *First, Break All the Rules* in 2000, many companies shifted away from the idea that accountability drives performance to a belief that engagement was the panacea, so they created committees and asked employees what would make them more engaged. Employees did not hold back. They called for raises, more time off, higher staffing levels, incentive awards, and many other self-serving desires. In the spirit of employee engagement and hopes of great ROI, the employers delivered. Employee satisfaction skyrocketed; however, they did not get engagement—they got entitlement. Employees came to expect perks as reward for showing up every day.

After the economic downturn in 2008, companies could no longer afford to keep up the charade. It was quickly apparent that we needed a new tack to drive performance.

In 2010, Cy Wakeman published her best-selling book, *Reality-Based Leadership: Ditch the Drama, Restore Sanity to the Workplace, and Turn Excuses into Results*. After reading this book, I came to a striking realization: true engagement (not just satisfaction) yields results when employees hold themselves personally accountable.

Bam! There it is. As an integral part of an engagement strategy, employees should learn to point their finger toward themselves. Cy teaches that you need to stop fighting reality. "Your current circumstances are not the reason you can't be successful; it is the very reality in which you must be successful."

If you are interested in learning more about marrying engagement and personal accountability, I highly recommend looking Cy Wakeman up, or reading her newest book *No Ego: How Leaders Can Cut the Cost of Workplace Drama, End Entitlement, and Drive Big Results.*

THRIVING ORGANIZATIONS ARE RESILIENT

No one could have accurately predicted the recent cataclysmic natural disasters alongside widespread health, social, and economic emergencies. Luckily, behavioral science studies provide insight into predictable human responses to the crises we face.

In times of great anxiety, it is human nature to long for the comfort of the past, even when the past wasn't that great. During times of extreme or prolonged anxiety, Eddie (or whatever you have named your inner voice) kicks into high gear. His (or her or their) critical mission is to successfully guide us through the danger—in other words, to help us survive. And our psyche is keenly aware that we successfully navigated the past and therefore desires a return to the familiar.

When humans become increasingly fearful of the current reality (as we are now), our subconscious tends to recall memories that evoke feelings of great comfort or stability. Nostalgia is a strong psychological coping mechanism.

During the early stages of the pandemic, it became clear that most of society was hungry for simpler times. Stores quickly sold out of fishing poles, and many families dusted off old board games. In my house, we taught our teenage boys how to play Spades (the card game that consumed much of my freshman year in college). In the months since, we have developed a strong rivalry of parents vs. kids.

When Eddie realizes that a threat is not diminishing quickly, he has another trick up his sleeve. Because things feel out of control, he instructs us to take control in any way possible. Although most of us can understand the need for control during a crisis, it is rarely an effective coping mechanism.

For example, over the past decade I have refined my career by facilitating hundreds, if not thousands, of workshops and seminars. I had structured my business around conference and event hosting. My teammates and I operated like a well-oiled machine (for the most part). We would travel from city to city and state to state, building a coalition of like-minded business professionals. They say that if you do what you love, you will never work another day in your life. I had turned my dream into a reality.

But with the onset of COVID, I had to cancel all our upcoming events. Not only were my dreams dashed, but my income was also squashed. But I pride myself on being resilient. So, I got busy starting over. The plan was to reinvent my approach and go virtual. I purchased a Zoom webinar subscription and a high-quality video camera and microphone.

As I was preparing for my first online event, I saw a news story about "room rating"—a snarky (but funny) practice of shaming people on Twitter by rating their virtual background as *hot* or *not*. Apparently, this had become a thing.

Well, Eddie quickly informed me that I needed to take control of "my room" and prepare a suitable background. He also told me that if the background was perfect, my business (and career) would be saved. But what is a perfect background? I had never done this before. My growing need for control totally took over my sense of reason.

I spent an entire day arranging and rearranging the books on my shelves. I was obsessed with organizing the genre and color scheme. I searched the house for plants and picture frames to consume any open spaces. I found a pottery piece that I had purchased recently at Menards. I carefully placed the pot on the middle shelf of the case. I was disappointed when it appeared far too big for the spot. But I loved this piece; the color and style were perfect. I happened to recall that Menards had the same color and style in different sized pots. I grabbed my mask and went off to Menards with my husband. I was determined to create the perfect room and this smaller pot would seal the deal.

However, Menards was sold out of the size that I wanted. All at once my illusion of control collapsed. I had a legit meltdown in the garden aisle at Menards. My poor husband had no clue what was happening. *If I didn't have the perfect pot, everyone would room shame me . . . I would never work in this town again . . . I would become destitute and my children would starve.* Overdramatic I know, but that's how Eddie rolls.

I have since come to my senses, but I still rearrange my room background at least once a week.

I have observed this same phenomenon in countless organizations as they attempt to adapt to the demands of their new not-so-normal. We all were hit in the knees by the sh%#@storm of 2020.

Organizational norms are a product of human psychology. Our individual nature drives collective behavior.

The desire for the stability of the past and the need to gain greater control are also the coping methods of groups in the face of fear and anxiety. Therefore, it is only natural for an organization to revert back to survival mode in times of crisis.

I am currently working with more than one organization that regressed from thriving mode to surviving mode almost overnight. They immediately put all culture work on pause and began to look at situations through a command-and-control lens. GSD (get stuff done) became the overarching priority.

Being strategic has been replaced with being incredibly busy. The unspoken mantra has become "If your hair isn't on fire, you aren't working hard enough."

This backstep is understandable, but most companies are now realizing it is not sustainable. The hurdles that sent them on their evolutionary path in the first place—silos, disengagement, resistance, snarkyness, disempowerment, confusion, absenteeism, turnover—all resurfaced.

But there is good news: they can bounce back without navigating through a period of *striving*. They have already done that work. They have cleared the trail toward *thriving* and they can follow the breadcrumbs they have laid. Resilience will determine the speed at which they progress.

Thriving companies are notorious for expecting greatness. The concept of settling for "acceptable" results is unacceptable. However, they resist the norm to set and cascade lofty annual goals. Leaders in these companies realize that success is no longer a yearlong marathon; it is a series of fifty-two relay races.

When faced with unforeseen challenges, thriving companies do not lower their standards; they diligently focus on building greater resilience.

Marcus Buckingham and the ADP Research Institute (ADPRI) recently conducted a global study of resilience. They interviewed 25,000 working adults from twenty-five different countries. They found that only 19 percent of workers in the US exhibit high levels of resilience as measured against real-world stresses that are prevalent parts of the current working environment.

While coaching an executive of an aerospace manufacturing company, I discovered that the owner was prone to sharing success stories and downplaying challenges. He believed that bad news could jeopardize team morale and good news promoted motivation. He and his leadership team failed to realize that employees can see right through the curtain of positivity. The production team was fully aware of missed deadlines, customer complaints, and reduced revenues. The fact that the leaders were not communicating the reality of the situation was causing doubt about the company's stability.

I encouraged the leaders to share their pains as well as their gains. Employees value transparency. If you can trust them with the truth in difficult times, they are apt to respond with great resiliency.

Psychologist Viktor Frankl theorized that our response to unavoidable suffering is one of the primary sources of meaning, purpose, and self-efficacy in our lives. He deemed that suffering and difficulty must never be hidden. Instead, when shown honestly and clearly, others will reveal their greatest strengths.

In an article posted by *The Guardian*, "The psychology of luck: how superstition can help you win," Olga Oksman details the influence of lucky charms on resilience. She writes:

"Stuart Vyse, psychologist and author of *Believing in Magic: The Psychology of Superstition* found that people perform better on tasks when they have a lucky charm with them. In one study in 2010, researchers had students putt a golf ball. Half the students were told that the golf ball they were using was lucky. The students who thought they were putting with a lucky ball were better at it than students told they were using a regular ball.

"As part of the same study, a group of students who had lucky charms were recruited for a series of memory tasks. Half the students were allowed to keep their lucky charms with them, and the other half had their charms taken away. The students who were allowed to keep their charms performed better. In a skilled activity, lucky charms boost confidence for people who believe in them.

"Maia Young, associate professor at the UCLA Anderson School of Management explains ... Even though many people might not know how their lucky charms actually work, it is not a bad idea to carry a charm for added confidence.

"Personality and attitude play into luck as well. In her research, Young finds that optimism is positively associated with luck. If someone believes that they are lucky, and believes that good things will happen, they will try harder at a task.

"When people view themselves as lucky, they are more likely to choose and persist at challenging tasks.

"That persistence can have a self-reinforcing effect. The more challenging tasks people take on, the more chance there is they will succeed at some of them, giving them a sense that they are indeed lucky."

Interesting, but do lucky charms increase employees' resilience in the aftermath of 2020? I'm not sure, but I've been told that some leprechauns believe that they're "magically delicious."

However, in the ADPRI report, Marcus Buckingham provides more practical strategies to improve resiliency in the workplace.

He describes resiliency as the "capacity of an individual to withstand, bounce back from, and work through challenging circumstances or events at work."

The study found that "people's personal level of resilience in the workplace is closely related to their immediate team leader and their organization's senior leaders."

Marcus provides further confirmation:

- Loving the work you do each day is a contributing factor to being highly resilient.
- Trust in one's team leader is highly related to anticipatory communication and psychological safety.
- Resiliency is higher in workers who strongly agree senior leaders are one step ahead of events and always do what they say they are going to do.

Interestingly, in her article "Friday the 13th: How it came to be and why it's considered unlucky," CNN's Marika Gerken writes:

"1 in 4 Americans say they are superstitious. While the other 3 out of 4 Americans might scoff at this, there is actually psychological science to back superstition. Psychologists at Kansas State University say superstitions are all about trying to control your fate. People often use superstitions to try to achieve a desired outcome or to help alleviate anxiety."

This subconscious phenomenon can be compared to that of a baseball player who attributes his homerun streak to a certain pair of underwear. The undergarment may not carry any special qualities, but his psychological belief in its powers can actually fuel further success.

Gerken also states:

"One 2010 study conducted by psychologist Stuart Vyse tested a group of people on various memory tasks. The group of people who were allowed to carry their lucky charms with them performed better on the memory tests than the people who had their lucky charms taken away. 'It's all about that "low cost" confidence booster,' Vyse concluded."

In thriving organizations, inspiration has replaced the need for motivation. Efforts to inspire, which lead to intrinsic motivation, clearly outweigh any performance incentives.

INNOVATION

Strategic HR Leaders challenge convention, look to the future, and manage change. We utilize technology, social science principles, validated research findings, and changing market trends to deliver proactive HR strategies.

WHAT IS INNOVATION?

When most people hear the word "innovation," they naturally think about digital technology. Sure, technology is a component of innovation, and an intuitive HRIS and emerging AI are valuable tools to collect data and deliver employment solutions. If your current systems are not user-friendly or fail to provide critical data, you may want to conduct a needs analysis and explore options. However, innovation goes far beyond just tech solutions.

You are probably constantly bombarded with articles about HR transformation, disruption, redesign, or streamlining. There are countless consultants touting countless methods to guide you on this "innovation" journey. They all claim to have a proven model to implement a more efficient alignment of the people and business strategies. However, thriving companies know that no calculated process will drive change without an appetite for progress.

Innovation is not simply a practice; it starts as a mindset. Embracing innovation requires the courage to take risks, an eye for possibilities, a fascination with novelty, a passion for ideation and exploration, and a curiosity about the future.

Innovation does not follow a calculated set of rules or tasks. It often leads to incremental failures, but it can also lead to small and even monumental improvements that can greatly elevate your mission.

Change is rapid, dynamic, and prevalent in the current business climate. Thriving organizations are those that are quick to adapt. Knowing that innovation is an imperative lever for success, savvy leaders have upgraded every aspect of doing business . . . except how they manage people.

WHY HR HAS FAILED TO EVOLVE

Any rational person would agree that the workplace has drastically changed over the past 150 years. However, the management principles established by Fayol and Taylor are still held as best practice today. Daniel Pink describes management as an invention, similar to that of the television. But he recognizes that the concept is treated more like a tree, which is an enduring fact of nature.

I believe there are several reasons why our people management model has failed to evolve while other business practices have been modified with the rapidly changing business landscape.

First, there is the overwhelming gravity of failure. Innovation requires considerable trial and error, and this can be a dangerous proposition in the face of people practices.

Human resources professionals are typically cautious in nature—with good reason. After experiencing considerable pain—emotional, physical, or even *professional*—it is human nature to actively avoid similar circumstances. This is very true for HR. Too often, HR is not consulted on problematic situations until the proverbial poop has hit the fan . . . the stakes are elevated, and the implications are painful. In the wake of such occasions, the impact on HR's future decision-making is vastly skewed toward prevention of the same. Naturally, this makes us highly trepidatious when exploring novel approaches.

Second, if there is widespread belief that command and control is an essential (tree-like) component of any functional workplace, most will resist alternatives.

Cognitive dissonance is the psychological impact when a person is faced with contradictions to what they believe to be true. This discomfort leads to one of three eventual resolutions:

- **Dismissal of facts.** To relieve the psychological discomfort of cognitive dissonance, an individual may simply deny the existence or validity of realities that are in conflict with their personal truths. America has been experiencing this phenomenon with great frequency over the last few years. The idea of "fake news" is a manifestation of the cognitive dissonance created by conflicting ideologies.
- **Dismissal of source.** Another strategy to relieve the

dissonance is to question the intentions or credibility of the person(s) presenting the conflicting information. This allows the subconscious to justifiably retain the conflicting belief. When implementing changes in the workplace, buy-in from stakeholders is desirable; however, we are often given tongue-in-cheek declarations of acceptance, only to eventually experience resistance or actual sabotage.

- **Self-reflection.** This tactic—the most effective—requires a higher degree of emotional intelligence. In the throes of cognitive dissonance, reflection requires us to examine our personal truths through the lens of a conflicting reality. We must ask ourselves, "With this new perspective, is my personal truth still serving me well?" Then a pragmatic analysis of the situation will greatly calm the psychological discomfort.

Third, we try to manage change. But change can't be managed; it is coming whether we are ready or not. The real objective is for all on the team to think proactively and continually adapt.

Because I live in Minnesota, I think this concept is best described in weather-related terms. A blizzard is a very disruptive event. When the snow and strong winds arrive, they can shut down even the sturdiest business practices. There is always a major storm in our future. However, we can't manage when it will hit or how long it will last; we must prepare to mitigate the impact (or embrace the opportunities) it brings. It would simply be malpractice to accept business losses as the result of a snowstorm. Thriving Minnesota organizations long ago discovered adaptations and innovations to keep balls rolling during the long winter season.

If innovation is to become an embedded characteristic of a thriving culture, you must anticipate and navigate the certainty of cognitive dissonance. As a leader, you will need to lead others toward self-reflection. This may require you to challenge the following belief: "In order to innovate, I must help others become more comfortable with change." Get ready for your own cognitive dissonance when I tell you that *comfort* should not be the goal.

Cognitive dissonance is an integral component of innovation. Eddie will always view any change as a threat (I know, Eddie is a jerk). Eddie fully understands that you can survive what is already known, the status quo. However, there is no guarantee of surviving the unknown, change. As a result, most changes are psychologically processed as a "scary" proposition. Change is uncomfortable, but this is not a bad thing. If you focus on cultivating comfort, change—and with it a culture of innovation—will be elusive. Comfort is derived from the *lack* of change. It is impossible to avoid the emotional swamp on the innovation path. You can't go around it; you must go through it. It is your responsibility as a leader to ensure others keep swimming and reach the other side as soon as possible.

While trying to manage change (and reduce discomfort), we have sent the unintended message that employees have the discretion to opt in or opt out of change initiatives. To quote author and speaker Cy Wakeman, "Buy-in is not optional." If a team member is struggling with cognitive dissonance, you may need to facilitate greater self-reflection. However, if they cannot find a way to get on board, then they will need to leave the team. Continued resistance will lead to unnecessary drama and the delay of innovation.

THE PERFORMANCE MANAGEMENT PARADOX

I have facilitated hundreds of Strategic HR workshops. One of my favorite activities asks participants to consider the value of certain conventional wisdoms. When presented with a statement about a commonly held HR maxim, respondents choose to either move to the left of the room to signify their agreement or navigate to the right in disagreement.

When presented with the statement "The traditional annual performance review is the best tool to improve employee performance," the group largely congregates to the right. Then I instruct members of the group to raise their hand if they conduct annual performance reviews. Usually a majority of the right-sided group sheepishly raise their hands. The irony of this paradox is not lost on the group.

A spirited conversation ensues when I probe further. I ask the group why they continue to pursue a very costly process, year after year, when they don't believe it is the best tool to improve performance. I hear many explanations, but by far the most common response is "We need documentation in case any issues are litigated down the road."

I understand the comfort that documentation provides for the wary HR manager, but this premise is misguided.

When—not if—a disgruntled employee approaches an employment attorney with their grievance, you will quickly discover that your documentation isn't the saving grace you thought it would be. Most attorneys will take on a wrongful termination or employee discrimination case whether it is substantiated or not. Why? Because the odds are stacked in the employee's favor.

Many attorneys will argue a case on a contingency basis, which means the employee does not need to pay any legal fees to file the suit, so the employee has nothing to lose. However, the employer has everything to lose: their reputation, their employer brand, money, and considerable staff hours. Savvy lawyers understand that the defendants are highly motivated to settle these cases without going to court.

In this case, your documentation will not matter. You may have proof that all involved did everything by the book and it will rarely change the outcome. It is well advised to make the case go away as quietly as possible.

But in the rare event that your case does go in front of a judge, your documentation can hurt more than it can help. Any qualified lawyer can spin any document to support any argument, therefore negating HR's comfort.

Redesigning people and talent management practices is a critical step of any organization's evolutionary journey. Strategic HR Leaders must discover methods that meet the needs of the modern workplace, and the best place to start is with performance management.

Although performance management is a broad topic, let's start by dissecting the traditional review. Spoiler alert: I believe the practice of filling out a form with a supervisor's rating of each direct report's performance against a set of ambiguous competencies and meaningless goals that were set twelve months prior should be sent through a woodchipper, thrown in the trash, set on fire, and never spoken of again. Let's explore why.

HR typically looks to the annual review to objectively evaluate performance, determine wage increases, validate promotions, provide good feedback, set goals, identify learning opportunities, justify disciplinary action, initiate coaching conversations, and inevitably, improve performance. How can a single process, which is despised by every supervisor and employee, be expected to accomplish so much? Simple—it can't.

The performance review also poses a few ideological problems. First, humans are not good raters of other humans. In the 2015 article "Most HR Data Is Bad Data" posted by the *Harvard Business Review*, Marcus Buckingham writes:

"Over the last fifteen years a significant body of research has demonstrated that each of us is a disturbingly unreliable rater of other people's performance. The effect that ruins our ability to rate others has a name: the Idiosyncratic Rater Effect, which tells us that my rating of you on a quality such as "potential" is driven not by who you are, but instead by my own idiosyncrasies—how I define "potential," how much of it I think I have, how tough a rater I usually am. This effect is resilient—no amount of training seems able to lessen it. And it is large—on average, 61% of my rating of you is a reflection of me.

"In other words, when I rate you, on anything, my rating reveals to the world far more about me than it does about you. In the world of psychometrics this effect has been well documented. The first large study was published in 1998 in *Personnel Psychology*; there was a second study published in the *Journal of Applied Psychology* in 2000; and a third confirmatory analysis appeared in 2010, again in *Personnel Psychology*. In each of the separate studies, the approach was the same: first ask peers, direct reports, and bosses to rate managers on a number of different performance competencies, and then examine the ratings (more than half a million of them across the three studies) to see what explained why the managers received the ratings they did. They found that more than half of the variation in a manager's ratings could be explained by the unique rating patterns of the individual doing the rating—in the first study it was 71%, the second 58%, the third 55%."

This is highly problematic when you consider the brevity and consequence of performance ratings. Performance ratings are often used to justify wage decisions and to elevate—or ruin—careers.

Many well-meaning HR practitioners have failed to overcome this phenomenon despite efforts to calibrate rating criteria and force a bell curve. Even GE, notorious for its long-held commitment to a forced ranking system, has dumped this flawed practice.

This process almost always produces a threat response, and Eddie doesn't care about performance; he eagerly exploits one's cognitive dissonance to deflect the sting of any rating below a five.

I recently witnessed an annual review meeting that presented 360-degree performance feedback from peers, customers, and direct reports of a very capable and accomplished manager.

Although 95 percent of the feedback was very flattering, 5 percent described ways in which the respondents believed she could improve her performance. This leader, who was usually fairly confident in her abilities, was crushed. She obsessed on the negative feedback for weeks, and her confidence and performance suffered. She logically agreed that the feedback was valid and helpful, but she could not get around the betrayal she felt.

There is very little evidence that the traditional performance evaluation process is tied to improved performance. Often the converse is true. Even when meaningful goals are set for the upcoming year, they are often obsolete or forgotten by the next month. Around month eleven, employees are forced to rush to make some progress toward an objective that is no longer relevant.

There is evidence, however, that this is a very costly process and admittedly hated by almost all, including HR. I have had a few remarkably interesting conversations with Roger Ferguson, author of *Finally! Performance Assessment That Works: Big Five Performance Management.* He suggests that companies (namely HR) need to calculate the ROI of their performance management practices. He shared that in his consulting practice he has helped many organizations do just that and the findings were predictable.

The traditional model requires managers to spend countless hours formulating and documenting justification for the performance ratings given to each and every direct report. I have met managers who have spent an entire month going through this routine because they have over fifty employees on their team. Managers tell me that they are just going through the motions, but they see little if any impact on productivity or efficiency. Often, they report a decline in performance after the review meetings.

We must finally admit that the actual cost and the opportunity costs are too burdensome, and that the ROI of performance reviews is virtually nonexistent.

However, after acknowledging the shortcoming of the annual review, many of the HR folks in my workshops report that they intend to continue their established protocols. Why? Because there is not yet a suitable alternative. This is the paradox.

Therefore, you must innovate.

If you do some research, you can find a lot of valuable studies and some great evidence-based practices put out there by many progressive thought leaders. But I highly suggest that you begin looking at performance management through a new lens.

Although it is still critically important for HR to mitigate the organization's risk exposure, you need to stop depending on the performance review and progressive discipline to provide legal cover. If you want to design talent solutions that managers will use and employees will appreciate, you need to focus on three very distinct, yet interrelated, talent management objectives: evaluation, elevation, and compensation. Accomplishing these objectives in tandem will require multiple solutions.

EVALUATION

When designing performance *evaluation* solutions, you need to ensure that they reflect real performance. Because the idiosyncratic rater effect proves that a categorical rating scale fails to capture an accurate picture, we need to tap into the insights of the person closest to the work: the employee themselves. Many of you probably already utilize self-evaluations, but the information collected is designed to be validated, challenged, or dismissed by the supervisor.

I can almost hear your thoughts . . . you are worried that employees will inflate their contributions to look better. I understand why this concerns you. In a command-and-control culture, it is in the employee's best interest to impress their boss in hopes of getting a good performance rating that results in a generous raise. So, in this environment employees could be tempted to exaggerate their performance.

But I have found the opposite to be true more often than not. Most employees tend to downplay their own successes and focus mostly on the great efforts of their team. When given the chance to do the right thing, employees usually will. But to encourage candid, holistic, and accurate depictions, this process should not have any impact on the employee's compensation in any way. We'll talk more about merit-based comp (pay for performance) later in this chapter.

Any self-evaluation process should be simple enough not to annoy, complex enough to capture a broad scope, and reflective of the organization's desired culture.

I am currently working with a non-profit organization that has defined their desired culture based on the following beliefs:

- "We believe that employees thrive when they regularly utilize their unique strengths."
- "We believe we win or lose as a team; relationships matter."
- "We believe that good coaching fuels employee engagement and high performance."
- "We believe that personal leadership drives improvement."

Although the culture project plan spans a period of three years, we redesigned the evaluation process in year one. To my delight—and that of every manager—we threw out their evaluation form. It has consisted of a multipage document in which managers were required to write a justification for the rating given to an employee's performance over a broad array of ambiguous competencies. We replaced it by asking each employee to tell their performance story by providing recent examples of times when they did the following:

- Used critical thinking to solve a problem
- Collaborated with teammates to deliver an outcome
- Demonstrated personal leadership in the workplace

Employees were asked to reach out and share their performance stories with their supervisor. Not to seek validation or approval, but to offer a true depiction of their efforts. Although several employees were trepidatious, I am happy to report that the new process was widely appreciated. Some managers reported that they had to push a few employees to brag about their accomplishments a bit more, but none of them requested a return to the old methods!

The organization even asked their communications manager to facilitate workshops for any employees who wanted help writing their story.

We explained that managers could ask questions and discuss the stories, but that this conversation was to be directed by the employee. Managers were encouraged not to point out any shortcomings or "areas of opportunity" at this time.

Part of the objective was to move away from command and control and promote personal accountability. We wanted to take the burden off the manager and ask the employees to own the process. We explained that they were not mandated to reach out and share with their manager, but if they didn't, we would assume that their performance story was not a positive one.

Although this novel approach is an employee-led process, the manager's perspective is still critically important. You may not ask for their idiosyncratic ratings, but you do need to tap into their views. I suggest asking managers to rate their own level of confidence in each team member. This should be viewed as an insight into the manager's opinion (which you should trust and value or they should not be a manager), not an evaluation of anyone's actual performance.

Another evaluation tactic is to propose this hypothetical scenario to each member of a team: If you were asked to lead a special project for the next month, which three teammates would you ask to join the team, and why? Again, this gives you insight from each team member without asking them to evaluate the competency of others.

Utilizing these tools can provide a well-rounded albeit subjective (because full objectivity is unattainable when you are dealing with humans) performance profile for each employee and team. This insight will enable you to calculate the HR-ROI. Below you will find a new 9-Box in which you can graph each member at the intersection of their performance (low, average, or high) and the employer's investment in the employee (low, average, or high).

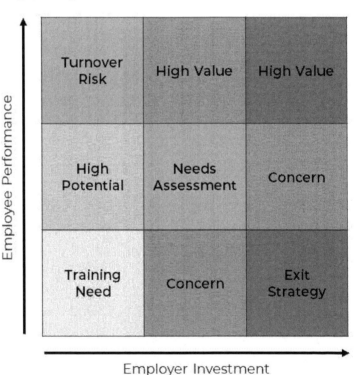

Figure 2: HR 9-Box (Copyright 2020 Ideation Consulting, LLP)

ELEVATION

As you design your talent *elevation* solutions, the 9-Box can help pinpoint your organization's talent strengths and weaknesses.

If you imagine a black line traveling from the lower left corner to the upper right corner, this is the line of neutral HR-ROI. Above the line depicts a positive HR-ROI, and below the line reflects a negative HR-ROI.

Obviously, it is desirable to move employees toward the high value areas. You have heard the adage that managers (and HR reps) spend 80 percent of their time coaching the bottom 20 percent of performers. This is unfortunately true. It is human nature to want to move the folks in the lower three brackets up the graph, but that is not always the best use of your talent elevation resources.

Let's suppose Bobby has been slotted below the black line. His salary is high in comparison to his peers, but his contributions lag behind those of his teammates. Although it would move him left on the investment axis, you never want to lower anyone's wages in this situation. Therefore, it seems intuitive to take action that will move Bobby up the performance axis. But first you need to ask yourself a question: If I invest more time, effort, energy and talent elevation resources (which will move him further right on the investment axis), am I fairly confident that his performance will move him into the positive HR-ROI zone? If the answer is yes—because he hasn't been given adequate training, or the right equipment or some other reasonable factor—get busy developing an appropriate talent elevation plan with Bobby.

However, if you don't believe these investments will move Bobby above the black line, you have a serious decision to make.

Again, additional talent elevation resources will push his point on the investment axis further right, resulting in a higher point of neutral HR-ROI for Bobby. This strategy will most likely prevent him from being fired (for now), but it fails to raise him into the positive HR-ROI zone.

Now I am not advocating that you ignore Bobby or fire everyone in the negative HR-ROI area. But I do encourage you to invest a majority of your talent elevation resources in those employees who reside in the positive HR-ROI zone. This is the greatest opportunity for you to elevate the talent in your organization.

You are surely aware that effective talent elevation efforts require considerable involvement of the direct supervisor, but how can we help set managers up for success?

Let's pretend that you have just moved into your dream house. Maybe a cabin in the woods or a loft in the city. As you are moving in there is a knock at the door. Your neighbor, Fred Rogers (yes, that Mr. Rogers) has dropped by to welcome you to the neighborhood. You can't believe it; you have moved next door to the best neighbor in the history of neighbors.

Fred proceeds to tell you about all the great families in the neighborhood. He describes block parties and elaborate holiday decorations. You are overwhelmed with his kindness.

Following his warm welcome, Fred says, "Oh and by the way, I took the liberty of typing up this description of how you need to take care of your lawn. I have highlighted these ten tasks that must be completed every week. If you are unsure of the process, I would be happy to instruct you. If you need any tools, feel free to take any from my shed. After six months we'll sit down, and I will rate on a scale of one to five how well you're doing. If you get a four or five, we will celebrate with a BBQ. If you get a three or lower, I will need to put you on probation—and if you don't improve, you'll have to move out."

What?! How do you feel about Fred now? Do you still think you are lucky to have him as a neighbor? Why not? He was genuinely nice and helpful. As it turns out, there are neuropsychological reasons why you want to kick him in the teeth.

The adolescent brain thrives with command and control. Young people need parents, teachers, and other authority figures to tell them what, when, where, and how to do things. Children learn quickly from rewards and punishments. This is what psychologists describe as the parent-child relationship. By design there is an imbalance of power.

However, in early adulthood our brains begin to change. With maturity we start to crave autonomy, freedom, and independence (thank goodness or our kids would live with us forever). The adult brain actively rejects command and control.

Mr. Rogers turned what should be an adult-adult relationship with a balance of power into that of a parent-child relationship defined by command and control. Sound familiar?

The adult brain seems all but primed to wholly reject a boss's authority. The idea of a reporting structure automatically establishes an imbalance of power. The superior has power over the wages, career opportunities, and continued employment of the subordinate. Because the adult human brain rebels against this premise, managers are set up for failure on day one. So, what's the answer? Coaching!

If we employ supervisors to manage others, shouldn't the success or failure of the team be a direct reflection of the supervisor's performance? In thriving organizations, the role of the supervisor is often superseded by the adoption of a coaching model. The main accountabilities for the coach are governed by the accomplishments of the team. When employees genuinely believe that their coach's success is dependent upon the team's success, a balance of power will naturally follow.

We need to rethink how we define the role of the supervisor. Most managers have great technical and work coordination skills, but many need more support to deliver great coaching. More on this in the next chapter.

We have covered evaluation and elevation talent solutions; now let's discuss compensation.

COMPENSATION

Just like the decoupling of evaluation and elevation talent solutions, in my opinion, compensation decisions should stand alone. When you tie pay to ratings and depend upon the promise of raises to motivate performance improvement, the only thing employees focus on is the amount of the raise. Employees then see their worth as commensurate with their wages.

The human brain's reward response triggers a hormone cocktail that stimulates feelings of joy. But this is fleeting. When an employee receives a wage increase, they surely experience a reward response, but then the brain raises the stakes. To recreate the same feeling, the next trigger must be greater than the last. Employees come to expect larger increases year after year to revalidate their sense of worth.

HR is understandably hyperfocused on wage competitiveness. One of our primary jobs is to attract and retain talent, and compensation is a significant piece of the puzzle. I have witnessed many HR professionals request a sizable increase in the budget to cover annual market-based adjustments and merit increases. However, they often fail to consider the HR-ROI in their proposal.

Look back at the new 9-Box. Increased wages equate to higher employer investment, and the black line rises accordingly. If you calculate a wage budget on market analysis alone, you run the risk of moving the entire organization to the right and exponentially lowering the HR-ROI year after year.

I am not suggesting that you freeze wages; that would move employees toward the turnover risk box. However, I am suggesting that we look at compensation from a more strategic viewpoint.

When the proposed compensation budget is presented, any good CFO wonders what the return is on this increased investment. If our justification does not go beyond the desire to remain competitive, we have missed an opportunity to be a true strategic partner.

Before settling on your request, please consider (and be prepared to explain) the related implications.

After calculating the HR-ROI over the past twelve months, be prepared to identify the reasons for any variations. This, along with your talent elevation plan, will help you confidently predict the future HR-ROI. You need to be prepared to share how improved performance will not only offset the increased investment but will also elevate the HR-ROI.

But I understand the appeal of merit rewards. Please allow me to offer a few considerations.

Success is a team sport. I can't think of any modern job that doesn't require some form of collaboration or dependence on the efforts of others. Therefore, it makes sense to calculate team merit as opposed to individual merit. Work with the team to set and regularly measure KPIs, and then attach any rewards accordingly.

There are potential pitfalls with this approach. You must ensure that every employee is focused on elevating their contributions to the team's success. If you fail to address performance issues quickly, your high-value employees will become disillusioned.

Base salaries keep growing. Each time you give merit increases or make market-based adjustments to an employee's salary, their base salary grows. In subsequent years, merit increases get calculated off that new base, compounding over time. And since it is not advisable to reduce wages when the market shrinks, the base only goes up.

To moderate growth in base salaries, rather than making merit increases or market-based adjustments, consider awarding one-time, lump-sum payments (i.e., bonuses) instead.

Share the pains as well as the gains. Your merit pay program needs to include an affordability clause. If the organization's bottom line is trending down, you may want to freeze merit pay. Even if some teams hit their metrics, you can't afford to rob Peter to pay Paul.

Thriving organizations are quick to pivot when needed and foster an acceptance of risk taking. However, not every innovative solution works as expected. According to Megan McArdle in her best-selling book *The Upside of Down, Why Failing Well Is the Key to Success*, "Failure is fundamental . . . failure is the inevitable result of dynamic experimentation. Innovation is often the result of tough lessons learned and persistence."

DISTINCTION 5

INTEGRATION

Strategic HR Leaders truly understand the business drivers and collaborate closely with our non-HR colleagues to deliver practical human capital solutions that are highly valued throughout the organization.

FINDING A WAY TO YES

When I speak to senior leaders about their views of HR, they often describe how HR repeatedly applies the emergency brake when the operations team wants to make changes. Our colleagues respect our counsel and understand our desire to mitigate liability, but they also recognize the need to occasionally take calculated risks to stay ahead of the curve. To find a balance, HR needs to loosen our expectations from "perfect" to "reasonable."

This challenge is not necessarily an either-or proposition. We can forge a path to achieve mitigated risks *and* support operational changes. If we reconcile our cognitive dissonance and demonstrate our willingness to objectively consider the risk vs. reward ratio, we are more likely to be consulted earlier in the planning process.

I am often told that HR needs to increase our business acumen. What does that really mean?

Because of an overload of duties and responsibilities, HR staff often feels chained to their desks. But if we want to be strategic, we must leave our office regularly and engage with colleagues throughout the organization. If you inquire about their work and explore the challenges they face, you will gain considerable business acumen.

To be viewed as a strategic partner with business savvy, HR needs to cultivate strong relationships with the talent in the trenches. It is these hip-to-hip encounters that will provide you with the insights and credibility to offer practical talent solutions that will be useful and appreciated.

COACHING THE COACHES

When discussing talent development best practices, such as having managers coach rather than simply direct their direct reports, I often hear some variation of "That sounds great, Sara, but the managers in my company don't have the people skills to make this work."

Although they believe this is an immovable roadblock, I respond with the question "And who should do something about that?"

I agree that a large percentage of managers struggle with coaching. But HR needs to acknowledge our role in the existence and persistence of this disconnect. We are complicit in the promotion of talented practitioners with minimal assessment of their coaching abilities. Manager training usually covers the legal dos and don'ts, policy enforcement, and the progressive discipline process. We often fall short, however, in considering the needs of the team during this transition to a new manager. They tend to be anxious about the change and don't know what to expect from their new leader.

This is a generalization, of course, and I realize you may have evolved beyond this reality. But I would wager that a handful of managers in your organization have difficulty coaching effectively. As it turns out, it is HR who should do something about this. But no document wordsmithing, policy creation, form update, or protocol adjustment will turn a lackluster manager into a great coach. Instead, we need to get busy *coaching the coaches.*

Because we are the people experts, it is incumbent upon us to lead the coaching charge. I have found that managers don't understand coaching until they experience it. When HR demonstrates what a good coaching conversation looks like, lightbulbs slowly come on. As an HR professional, you are the best coach to coach a coach directly, but you are also the best coach to coach coaches on how to best coach . . . whew!

In other words, when managers come to you with concerns about an employee, don't just tell them how to handle the situation; show them how it's done. Accompany them to the coaching conversation. You may have to take the lead a few times, but when they are ready, you can start to hand over the reins.

When this plays out well, HR quickly goes from being viewed as the enemy to being appreciated as a valuable partner.

TEAM SPIRIT

Because success is a team sport, HR needs to collaborate with coaches to deliver solutions with the team dynamic in mind. Teams are no longer defined as just the folks who sit in the same area of the building, or only those who report to the same boss in a specific department. Today many teams are temporary and cross-functional by design.

Effective teams are a collection of employees with diverse strengths and expertise. I learned this lesson the hard way early in my career.

I was a corporate HR executive in a company with over 15,000 employees when the CEO tapped me to redesign the performance management system for the entire company. Needless to say, I was excited! This was the perfect project for me. I was going to be able to make a strategic impact in an area that I was certainly passionate about.

To begin this process, I assembled a team of brilliant colleagues to help. I asked eight coworkers from outside the HR department to join the project and scheduled two-hour committee meetings every week.

The initial meeting was high-spirited, and everyone offered great ideas. We explored many innovative options and considered the pros and cons of each. I knew we were off to a great start.

On week two, the committee eagerly gathered to share more thoughts and debate the merits of new ideas. Again, the committee members were very engaged and stayed out of the weeds.

However, when the meeting on week three turned into another brainstorming back-and-forth, I started to realize that we weren't really gaining any traction. Thinking through various ways to address the lack of progress, I decided it might be a good idea to have each team member take the Strengths-Finder assessment.

After studying the strengths themes of the group, I realized that I had recruited individuals who had strengths similar to mine. None of the profiles were exactly the same, but they all seemed to be strong strategists.

No wonder the planning had stayed in the clouds. That was everyone's strengths zone. When it came time to start implementing, there were no strong practitioners on the team to carry the ball.

I needed to pivot, so I thanked the team for their input and assured them that they would be included in any further strategic planning. Then I quickly assembled a strengths-diverse implementation committee.

To build cohesive teams, I have learned that you must start by considering the individuals. Like snowflakes and zebra stripes, each human is wonderfully unique. However, it is natural to assume that others think and see things the same way as you. This, of course, is a false belief. When teams fail to acknowledge the individuality of each teammate, drama often ensues.

I am often asked to come into an organization to do trainings about teamwork. Translation: please make these folks get along and stop the distracting drama. Cohesiveness is elevated when each member understands how others on the team make decisions, organize, and complete their work.

Take me for example: I truly enjoy sitting down and discussing all the variables and possible solutions to each and every situation. I love to explore the "what if" outcomes of all the possibilities. Only after a very in-depth look into my crystal ball can I express why I prefer any one particular idea over others. However, I can be easily influenced to change my mind by the thoughtful and/or provocative ideas of someone I trust and admire.

Through the years I have been labeled as "flighty," "having my head in the clouds," and "unfocused." However, this style works best for me. My personality demands that I engage in intellectual conversations and explore progressive ideas before I can develop a strategy, which usually proves to be the right decision for me.

My husband, on the other hand, has a very different approach to decision-making. I call him "the noodler." Whenever he is faced with a decision, he needs to research the issue, gather all related information, consult with all involved parties, and then spend a considerable amount of time reflecting on the options. Once he has come to a conclusion, he will then step forward and announce his position. I learned long ago that once he has landed, his mind is usually set.

I have been repeatedly called a procrastinator. However, I do not take it as an insult. Those who know me well understand that my best work is done in the eleventh hour. When I am pushed to complete a project ahead of deadline, I usually make numerous changes and only become satisfied with my work at 11:59. Because there is a widely held view that procrastinators are irresponsible, this trait has caused me some difficulties when working with a team.

I have never been accused of being overly organized. I work best in a loosey-goosey style. I am not deterred by chaos and I am uncomfortable with regimented agendas and itineraries. This can be particularly problematic when I am working with teammates who desire strong structure.

I once worked with a highly talented HR manager who was

the poster child for responsibility and organization. She was a fabulous yin to my yang. However, when we first met, I know I annoyed her greatly. One day she came to me and said she had finally realized that she needed to give me space to deliver my work. She admitted that she had often worried about my progress, even though I had reassured her there was no need to worry. "I was never sure if you would come through, but you always do," she told me. "I have learned that you will deliver greatness, but not until the last minute."

It is important for each team member to know that differences don't need to be judged as better or worse; sometimes they are just different.

Strategic HR Leaders understand the importance of effective collaboration. But it is the team leader who has the most influence over any team's success or failure. When you understand the unique dynamics of each team and forge a strong partnership with both the formal and informal team leaders, you will be best positioned to provide the appropriate team talent strategies.

PERFORMANCE DESCRIPTIONS

A few years ago, I was conducting an interview for a senior management role in a marketing company. After I gave the candidate a copy of the job description, he replied, "This is helpful, thank you. But can you please describe the contributions of someone who you would consider to be highly effective in this role?"

I was shocked (and impressed) by this unusual question. What I realized in that moment is that we, as an organization, had restricted our view of performance. We had obsessively detailed the minimum requirements for our employees. We had given each of them a formal document that clearly defined the steps they needed to take to be "good enough." But we had not informed them of what it would take to be a superstar (which is what we were ultimately longing for).

Different from a job description, a performance description is less an official document and more an opportunity to define good, great, and poor performance. It clearly describes the outcomes necessary to achieve excellence.

Outcomes can be looked at as the "fruits of our labor." Whereas the tasks and duties are the actual labor, the outcomes are the fruit (the sweet stuff). Few of us jump for joy when the proper procedures are followed, or the tasks are completed. However, we tend to celebrate wildly when we land a new client, set a new sales record, or complete a project on time and below budget. The outcomes are the "party-worthy" moments that we work so hard to achieve.

PERSONAL LEADERSHIP

When I ask managers to identify their superstars and describe what sets them apart, I regularly hear about those who accomplish amazing outcomes, but it is always accompanied by stories of demonstrably admirable character.

When discussing "problem" employees, managers often say things like "She is a great nurse, but patients tell us that she isn't very friendly" or "He is our good salesman, but he is rude to the administrative staff." Although these folks may be nailing the outcomes of their jobs, their teammates rarely consider them to be superstars because they lack personal leadership.

Personal leadership is not determined by title, position, or authority. It is indicative of emotional intelligence. Employees demonstrating personal leadership are described as having high integrity and empathy. They hold themselves accountable to high standards and are trusted by their teammates.

To elevate talent, coaches should help others examine their personal leadership strengths and weaknesses. Every employee can benefit from a professional development plan that clarifies strategies to improve critical thinking, collaboration, and personal leadership. Coaching conversations should include discussions about progress and challenges therein.

LOVING CANDOR

Good coaches realize that it is in every employee's best interest to be aware of anything that stands in their way of being wildly successful. They are not afraid to have difficult discussions, and they consider candor, the art of communicating real truths and honest impressions, to be a gift worth giving.

These tough conversations can be uncomfortable for even the most seasoned coaches. However, it is critical for employees to clearly recognize the realities of every situation. All too often, talented employees are unable—or unwilling—to face their own challenges. But, to quote Dr. Phil, "You cannot change what you do not acknowledge."

Every coach needs to master the art of loving candor. It can be uncomfortable, but true candor lifts the veil of denial. However, if the conversation ends there, cognitive dissonance and resentment are sure to follow. Relationship and dignity are preserved when candor is followed by a true commitment to help.

Loving candor has two objectives: encourage self-aware-ness and provide support in turning things around. This does not mean that you should jump in and solve the problem. Empathy and coaching are the ingredients to a lovingly candid conversation.

A few years ago, I was working on a development plan with an executive who is incredibly talented and successful. He is wildly admired in his profession and is revered by the business community. However, after completing several interviews with his team, I came to realize that many of his colleagues were growing frustrated with him because he was failing to follow through with his commitments.

I would often hear others whisper behind his back about his growing lack of respect for the team. This really bothered me because I knew how dedicated he was to his work and his coworkers. I decided to sit down with him to try to under-stand the situation. He informed me that he had taken on a new project that was consuming a large portion of his work time. He was engrossed in this exciting work, and he admit-ted to leaving loose ends with his other obligations. However, he failed to recognize the effect that this was having on his teammates.

As we continued our conversation, I realized that it was my duty to inform him of the negative consequences of his behav-ior. I told him that I was incredibly excited that he was working on such an important project, but I informed him that others were starting to question his dedication to the team. I candidly expressed their concerns and offered to assist him with rebuild-ing his quickly eroding relationships.

Although I felt uncomfortable (it would have been much easier to just congratulate him and sit back to wait for his approaching train wreck), I cared enough about this fellow to be honest with him.

EDDIE'S KRYPTONITE

During coaching conversations, it is common for managers to monopolize the dialogue. Many clearly present the facts and are quick to offer their assessment and guidance. However, to leverage the opportunity for learning, coaches need to be highly inquisitive.

Managers often have the expertise to readily solve most problems, but good coaches ask leading questions to help others come to the right conclusion themselves. Retention of learning is much greater when the lessons are self-realized as opposed to instructed.

Asking probing questions that encourage self-reflection is the best way to engage an employee's cognitive function without waking a sleeping Eddie. The most effective questions are void of judgment and accusation, thereby minimizing the threat response.

I have recently been coaching an HR manager in a smaller organization. She is one of the best coaches I have encountered. She is intuitively tapped into everyone's strengths and needs, highly empathetic, and fabulous at engaging others one-on-one. Relationship-building conversations seem to come very naturally for her.

However, when she interacts with members on the executive team, she clams up. She loses her confidence and waits passively for direction on what they would like her to do. She routinely misses opportunities to offer her valuable insights on a strategic level.

The other day I asked her, "Why do you interact differently with senior leaders than you do others?" Although surprised by the question, she acknowledged this reality and began a journey of self-reflection.

Through additional Q&A she realized that she felt intimidated by executives and more comfortable with peers. I further probed, "Why is that?"

I asked her to consider this question and we would discuss her thoughts the next day. After another great conversation, she agreed to embrace her vulnerability and have a long overdue conversation with the CHRO. If I had simply told her that she needed to talk to her boss, cognitive dissonance and Eddie wouldn't have allowed such profound growth.

STORY TIME

Humans learn best through stories. The brain gravitates to stories that describe a problem—or an antagonist—which, after much effort, is defeated by the hero of the story. Consider the nursery rhymes we read to our children at bedtime. Most are violent. Pigs' houses are blown down; witches put wayward kids in ovens; wolves threaten to eat girls wearing red riding hoods; and farmers' wives even cut off the tails of blind mice. When you think about it, that's some scary stuff to tell youngsters. But instead of becoming horrified, your little ones often beg for "just one more story" as you tuck them in.

Although the characters are anthropomorphic, the lessons from these tales are easily translated to the real world. This is the human brain's way of learning how to best navigate difficult situations without experiencing any actual physical, emotional, or psychological pain. These stories also stimulate imagination, creativity, and wonder.

Coaching stories aren't likely to include dancing pigs and talking wolves, but adults are psychologically impacted by stories of everyday heroes facing adversity. Great coaches tell stories of great challenges such as missed deadlines, mistakes, inefficiencies, or bad service, in which everyday heroes rose to the occasion—or sometimes stories of how lessons were learned through failure. The listener subconsciously connects the dots between the point of the story and their current realities. This approach hopefully keeps Eddie at bay, thereby providing a psychologically safe space to learn the hard lessons.

If you look back on the topics in this book, you probably won't remember most of the information I have included. But it is highly likely that the stories I have shared triggered a subconscious emotional response.

LEARNING STYLES

My father is a retired history/government teacher who spent the majority of his career at an inner-city high school in Des Moines, Iowa. He served on a special team that was charged with evaluating teacher skills. As a young girl, I witnessed my father's commitment to his students and his expertise.

At the dinner table one evening (I was probably around twelve years old), my father was imparting some of his wisdom (as he often did). He shared his knowledge of the sequential and global learning styles. I remember being captivated. The concept made so much sense to me. I clearly understood the concept and recognized myself as very much a global learner. That night

I gained valuable insight that would serve me well in my education and future career.

In a model introduced by Dr. Richard Felder and Barbara Soloman, learning distinctions are clearly defined. Although the theories are much more complex, the basic premise is useful for managers involved in training and development. From the article "Teaching Tip: Ways of Knowing – Sequential vs Global Learners" posted on the Vanier College website in November 2013:

Sequential learners learn best by understanding the details of a subject and slowly building an image of the bigger picture. Sequential learners work very well with details but often have trouble understanding larger concepts and ideas. You can help sequential learners by:

- Showing an outline or organized structure for the presentation of new material.
- Building your presentation of new material in steps that lead to the main concept or idea.
- Starting with simpler concepts and building up to more complex ideas.

Global learners need to see the bigger picture and how the new material connects to information they have already learned. Global learners work well with larger concepts or ideas but struggle with the details. You can help global learners by:

- Giving a short overview of the topic before jumping into the details.
- Drawing connections from specific details or information to the larger concepts.
- Having them work on problems or issues that encourage creative approaches rather than the application of a sequence of steps.

Although most managers are aware that there are differing learning styles, few understand these distinctions. When engaged in training, managers tend to teach from their own personal learning style as opposed to that of the trainee. This is mostly because it is difficult to assess individual learning styles. If you simply ask an employee their preferred learning method, it is unlikely that they will offer detailed insights.

When I work with managers, one of the first things I do is ask them to describe how they would assemble a piece of furniture delivered by IKEA or a bicycle to put under the tree on Christmas morning. If they are honest, sequential learners usually describe their task as follows:

1. Remove and read the assembly instructions.
2. Retrieve the necessary tools.
3. Verify the existence of all pieces.
4. Coordinate the pieces.
5. Follow the steps of assembly according to the instructions.

Sequential learners organize their thoughts in a linear, step-by-step manner. They function best when allowed to complete (and learn) each step one by one.

In contrast, global learners describe a different strategy. They usually start by looking at the picture of the finished product on the box. If a picture doesn't exist, they greatly benefit from a Google image search. They then jump in and intuitively put the pieces together and evaluate the accuracy in comparison to the photo. When they struggle, they may consult the instructions, but they tend to complete the steps in a random order.

I am a global thinker, and it amazes my sequential friends how much I struggle to follow a set of directions. If you are coming to dinner at my house and I am trying a new recipe, you should hope that there is a picture of the finished dish or things may go way off the rails. I find it almost impossible to complete a set of steps in sequential order. If I am given instructions with ordered tasks one through ten, I am likely to do #1, followed by #2 (with great effort to stay in order), but then jump to #6 and then review #10 in an attempt to better understand the final outcome. I know this sounds crazy to the sequential thinkers, but if you are a global thinker you totally understand.

Neither style is better or worse than the other; they are simply different. The point is that if you are a sequential thinker who is training a global learner, you need to adopt a global strategy, and vice versa. If you share the same learning style as the trainee, it might be helpful to have a conversation about the benefits and challenges of your style. But make no mistake, it is futile to attempt to change someone's dominant learning style (or your own). Smart people can adjust to the other method, but learning comes at a significant effort.

When conducting group workshops, I separate the room into the two groups—sequential and global thinkers—and ask everyone to pair up with someone from the other group. I then request that they describe to each other the way to erect a house of cards. It always amazes me how much confusion follows. I then ask them to do the same in a way that is more understandable to the other learning style and then check for learning. Afterward, we discuss how difficult it is to teach in the opposing learning style.

Coaching the coaches is the best and most expedient way to add value in your organization. If you can carve out time to exit your office and interact with managers and supervisors, you will develop strong relationships and establish the credibility that allows you to make a significant difference.

Pull Up a Chair

As I reflect on the research that led to the five distinctions of a Strategic HR Leader, I realize that if this research were conducted again today, we would likely discover the need for a sixth distinction: Inclusion.

After the death of George Floyd in my former Minneapolis neighborhood, the world finally took full notice of racial inequality issues. The subsequent protests elicited a visceral response. We collectively felt an obligation to do better.

HR leaders across the US and the world have always placed workplace diversity on the priority list, but the events that unfolded in the summer of 2020 elevated the urgency to achieve inclusion and equity. Our typical baby steps forward now seemed drastically insufficient.

Many employers released statements to publicly condemn racism and commit to activism. Notably, Best Buy released a joint statement from their executive team within days of the evolving tension in Minneapolis.

"Another black man in America died senselessly on Monday, and it happened only miles from where many of us live. As cars and people passed by, unaware that a man was struggling to breathe as another's knee was on his neck, our state and country witnessed yet another example of how the life of an African American man, woman, boy or girl is fundamentally different from their white friends, neighbors and colleagues.

"All this happened on the same day another black man, this time in New York City, was threatened by a white woman who said she would call the police on him when he requested she leash her dog, as required by city ordinance. She made that threat—and carried through on it—almost certainly knowing it would strike fear in the heart of any African American adult. She weaponized racism, and the whole world was able to watch.

"We write about these two events—and could certainly mention many more, including a young African American man chased and gunned down while jogging in southern Georgia—not because most of us know what this fear must be like. We are as a group, by and large, not people of color. We write this not because most of us have known anyone personally in a situation like this. Thankfully, most of us do not. We write this because it could have been any one of our friends or colleagues at Best Buy, or in our personal lives, lying on the ground, struggling to breathe or filming someone as they threatened us.

"This is the heart of the issue. Every time we see this kind of tragedy it can be hard not to feel emotional, not just for the human being affected or their family, but for the colleagues we know who could be—and have been—victims of overt, hostile and even dangerous racism. If we allow ourselves, it is not hard to imagine them lying on the ground begging to breathe or bravely staring racism in the eye as they walk through a park.

"If we permit it, we can—and we believe we should—see the moment for what it is: a horrific tragedy in Minneapolis or one in the making in New York City. But then we must take the next step, moving beyond it happening to a stranger to the possibility of it happening to someone we call a friend. Only then, in our view, do we begin to internalize how terrifying life can be for the black father or mother who must regularly remind their children what to do when facing a situation like this. Or what it must feel like for those same parents to know that they, too, could be facing it themselves.

"In keeping with our deep commitment to Diversity and Inclusion, the company will continue to invest resources and time on this topic, even in the face of the COVID-19 pandemic."

The letter was signed by CEO Corie Barry and all seventeen members of Best Buy's executive team.

Barry was quoted in the *Minneapolis/St. Paul Business Journal*:

"For me, it starts with seeing the situation for what it is, acknowledging these experiences for what they are and, quite simply, apologizing for not doing enough. As important, it includes committing the company I lead down a path of systemic, permanent change in as many ways as we can find."

In an interview published in the October 2020 issue of *HR Executive*, Ellyn Shook, the chief leadership & human resources officer of Accenture, committed to increase the representation of black workers from 9 percent to 12 percent and the representation of Hispanic and Latinx people from 9.5 percent to 13 percent. The company has also pledged to more than double the number of managing directors from those groups and to launch a new mandatory training to support workers in identifying and speaking up about racism. She was quoted:

"When George Floyd was killed, we continued to learn things about our workforce. We have an unwavering belief at Accenture that our diversity makes us smarter and more innovative. We want our people to be successful professionally and personally because when that magic happens, it's when you unlock the full potential of an organization. Race is a business issue."

HR YOU READY?

I understand that the messages throughout this book may be considered aspirational, but I believe it is past time to find our gravitas. We must redefine our profession and forge a strategic path for the HR leaders of the future.

While serving as an interim HR executive at a rural Oregon hospital, I met a dedicated young HR professional. Let's call her Sharon. She was very driven and juggled all the HR balls every day. Without the luxury of a robust HRIS, she was bogged down with inefficient processes that monopolized her time and energy.

Early in our relationship, I realized that Sharon was primarily a coach, secondarily a strategist, and lastly a practitioner. Focusing on administrative tasks for the majority of her day was depleting her and not leveraging her talents. However, the tasks were important and needed to remain a priority. After several conversations with Sharon, we proposed a plan to increase the hours of the part-time HR assistant, Sue.

Sue was a fabulous administrative practitioner. She was energized by organizing anything; she loved the process of turning chaos into order. It made sense to bring her in to streamline the processes that were weighing heavily on the team. However, we resisted the urge to tell her *how* to do it. We simply asked her to help, and she got busy applying her strengths to reduce the piles of files. Her smile and positivity were contagious.

With Sue streamlining the administrative tasks, Sharon was able to focus on coaching and engage in strategic conversations with me. She had never thought about HR as a strategic partner. As we discussed the importance of relationships with the managers throughout the organization, I watched her passion light turn on.

We worked together to define her role as a coach and strategic partner. Although she still needed to take care of some administrative tasks, her newfound strengths raised her credibility and visibility within the organization.

Eager to make a difference, Sharon had an epiphany one day. She had heard that the on-call staff were having issues with the nursing staff. They did not see eye to eye on when and why to call in assistance. Communication was lacking and relationships were being strained. Sharon decided to bring the two groups together to determine a process that would work for both. She did not fix the problem; she led the discussions. A compromise was reached without much further drama.

Sharon came to me after the meeting and said that she understood that coaching does not mean supervising; it means being a facilitator. It was fun to see her swim outside of her normal lane. She thanked me for being the first person to invest in her and her career.

Although I was proud, I was sad at the same time. I realized that many junior HR professionals probably have not experienced strategic mentorship. We simply can no longer depend on the traditional HR path—from assistant to recruiter to generalist/specialist to supervisor to manager to senior manager to executive—to provide the strategic insights our organizations so desperately need.

Traditional hierarchies create disincentives to mentor others. If I had been the permanent head of HR, it would have been a threat to my career for Sharon to leverage her coaching and strategic skills. If she became more impactful, what would my role be? This is the greatest failure of the organizational chart and traditional career pathing.

The majority of trainings and seminars available to HR professionals are dominated by employment law and compliance. They don't teach the distinctions of a Strategic HR Leader in college. You can't sit for the SPHR or SHRM-SCP exam until later in your career. Let's rethink how we support junior professionals.

To stay relevant and cultivate strategic talent solutions, HR needs to embark on a Leader*shift*. If we do not pivot, I am truly afraid that we will inevitably become obsolete. If our traditional contributions can be outsourced to providers that can do the work better and cheaper, we must seize the opportunity to forge the strategic role we have long coveted.

I hope this book has helped inspire you to start (or to continue) your Strategic HR Leadership journey and to mentor others along the way.

Resources

Overwhelmed? Remember that making a difference requires accepting difficulty and risk as essential stepping-stones on the journey.

But I want to help! I am energized by seeing strategic light-bulbs turn on like they did with Sharon. To that end, I have designed a professional development program to further explore the five distinctions. If you or your team would like more information, please visit www.hrleadershift.com, or email me at sara@ideation-consulting.com. We can arrange a video call to discuss opportunities or just talk "shop." I would love to hear your impressions of this book and answer any questions you may have.

Afterword

As I spend this Sunday evening making final edits to this manuscript prior to sending it off to my publisher in the morning, I am nursing a heavy heart. On Wednesday, a mob of rioters stormed the United States Capitol Building, injuring many and causing the death of five Americans. This is a direct assault on the principles of our democracy, but keep in mind the Capitol is also a *workplace*. Police officers, members of Congress, and hundreds of staff had reported to do the people's business. While performing their jobs, they were terrorized and their workspaces violated.

Whether you are a Republican, Democrat, or Independent, you should be concerned. Many identified rioters have subsequently been fired by their employers.

All employers need to consider the implication of these types of events and as HR Leaders I am afraid that we need to be prepared to address similar politically charged, contentious situations.

As we face the year ahead, the vaccine is on its way, the new administration is at the helm, and economic recovery is on the horizon. Like our country, I pray that your workplace is peaceful and collaborative. In the words of the late Minnesota Senator Paul Wellstone, "We all do better when we all do better."

Acknowledgements

I would like to thank a long list of people who helped make this book possible.

I must start with my husband and partner, Todd. Thank you for standing by me, even when my ideas seemed crazy. You are the love of my life, and I am so proud to be your wife. You have provided me with the opportunity to have it all. We have great kids, we have built a wonderful home, and because of you, I am able to chase my dreams every day. It hasn't always been easy, but it has been worth it. I love you.

To my two sons, I love you more than you will ever know. I marvel at the young men you are becoming. Thank you for granting me the space to pursue my dreams. I will always be by your side as you pursue yours. I am honored to be your mom.

To my mother-in-law and best friend, JoAnn, thank you. You are my role model. You have set a grand example of what it means to be a wife and mother while building a fulfilling career. I hope you realize how much I value your patience, your guidance, and your support. And to my father-in-law,

Jerry, I wish you peace. You never lost your sense of humor even in the darkest hours. I miss you every day.

To my big sister Sheila, thank you for being my constant ally. Together we have navigated many rough waters. The journey ahead is unknown, but with love and truth, I know we can weather any storm.

To my parents, thank you for Cookie Park, Crawdad Cove, and homemade Christmas tree decorations. You have taught me to value education, appreciate nature, and cherish one another in good times and in bad. Thank you for the bedrock on which I have built a beautiful life.

To the countless friends and colleagues who have stood beside me (you know who you are), I send infinite gratitude!

You may call it karma, fate, or shear randomness, but I believe people are divinely sent to intersect our lives at the times we need them the most. When I was writing this book, I googled *how long is the average nonfiction book?* I came across an article that answered my question eloquently. As I scrolled the text, I noticed the author's picture. OMG, it was my childhood friend Karin Wiberg.

Karin and I literally grew up together. From kindergarten to high school graduation, she and I shared most of life's experiences. We were Girl Scouts in the same troop, we performed in chorus and jazz choir together, and we even worked alongside one another at Baskin-Robbins. After graduation, our lives went in different directions, but I thought of her often.

So when I realized that Karin had founded her own publishing firm in North Carolina, I reached out immediately. She was exactly who I needed at the exact time I needed her. Not only is she now my publisher, but we have also renewed a valuable friendship. Thanks, Karin. (www.clearsightbooks.com)

ABOUT THE AUTHOR

During her twenty-plus-year career as a social scientist, Sara Christiansen has had the privilege to work with a diverse array of organizations in both the private and public sectors. As CEO and senior consultant at Ideation Consulting, Sara is responsible for designing customized organizational development solutions that drive true business results. She has a firm grasp of evidence-based talent development methodologies and facilitates strategic programs to help her clients maximize the return on their human capital investments.

Sara has vast experience working with professionals at all levels in an organization. Whether delivering a formal presentation to a room full of executives or providing one-on-one coaching for an emerging leader, Sara's passionate style allows her to connect with all audiences in a way that energizes individuals to perform at a higher level.

As preferred provider with the Society for Human Resource Management and the Human Resource Certification Institute, Sara travels throughout the United States to deliver strategic HR and business leadership programs.

Sara attributes her success to many factors, but she is especially proud of her ability to identify and embrace opportunities. She finds that grand possibilities stem from strong relationships. She says, "I often find myself in passionate exchanges with like-minded professionals. When I reach out to forge new connections, amazing opportunities often follow."

Sara has a degree in social science from Northwest Missouri State University and is a proud alum of the Delta Zeta Sorority. Today she lives in New Ulm, Minnesota, with her husband and two teenage sons. During the summer months, Sara can often be found at her lake cabin "up north."

Made in the USA
Columbia, SC
26 August 2021